# Frommer's®

D0052136

# 100

## Best Packing Tips

*by Kara Murphy*

WILEY

John Wiley & Sons, Inc.

# Contents

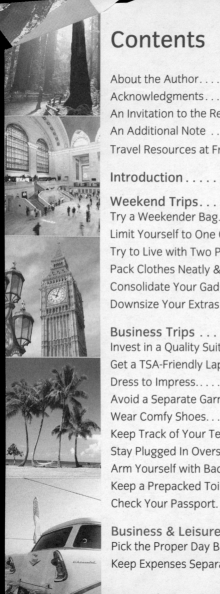

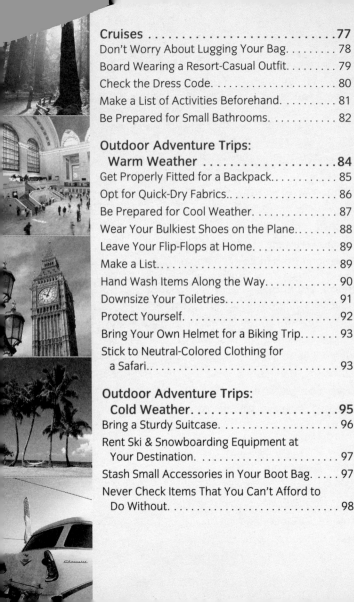

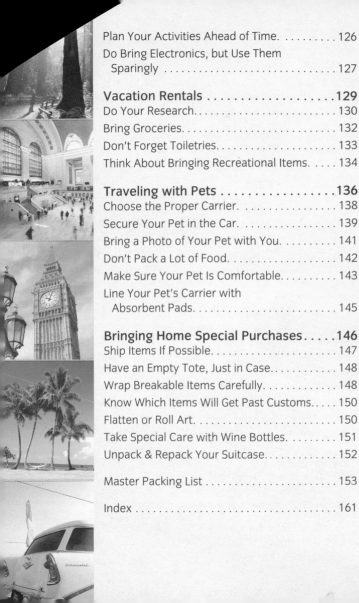

Published by:

# John Wiley & Sons, Inc.

111 River St.
Hoboken, NJ 07030-5774

ISBN 978-1-118-16494-5

Editor: Christine Ryan
Production Editor: Heather Wilcox
Photo Editors: Cherie Cincilla & Alden Gewirtz
Interior book design: Melissa Auciello-Brogan
Production by Wiley Indianapolis Composition Services

For information on our other products and services or to obtain technical support, please contact our Customer Care Department within the U.S. at 877/762-2974, outside the U.S. at 317/572-3993 or fax 317/572-4002.

Wiley also publishes its books in a variety of electronic formats. Some content that appears in print may not be available in electronic formats.

Manufactured in the United States of America

5 4 3 2 1

# About the Author

**Kara Murphy** (www.karakmurphy.com) is a freelance writer, reporter, and editor covering travel, fashion, beauty, consumer gadgets, and celebrities for several major magazines, websites, and publishing companies. At *People* and *People StyleWatch*, she wrote about the hottest new products and trends, flattering clothing and accessories for different body shapes, how to travel in style, and beauty secrets from industry pros (just to name a few!). While there, she also blogged for People.com.

Her passions include traveling, tracking down food trucks, vintage shopping, art, and indulging her inner geek as much as possible. Kara also enjoys spending her time organizing closets, flexing her double-jointed thumbs, and decorating her studio apartment with flea market finds (not necessarily in that order).

Kara holds a journalism degree from Northwestern University. She currently lives in Brooklyn, NY, but she loves to travel to her hometown of Tallahassee, FL whenever the humidity drops below 100%.

# Acknowledgments

I'd like to extend special gratitude to my family, friends, and colleagues for their boundless support, unfailing even when I decided to leave a steady gig to pursue a freelance career and dedicate more time to out-of-office adventures. I could not have made the leap without them.

I'd also like to thank everyone who patiently, and thoroughly, answered my questions as I pumped them for information about their packing rituals, advice, and absolutely genius tips.

# An Invitation to the Reader

In researching this book, we discovered many wonderful packing tips and tricks. We're sure you have more. Please tell us about them, so we can share the information with your fellow travelers in upcoming editions. If you were disappointed with a recommendation, we'd love to know that, too. Please write to:

*Frommer's 100 Best Packing Tips,* 1st Edition
John Wiley & Sons, Inc. • 111 River St. • Hoboken, NJ 07030-5774

# An Additional Note

Travel information can change quickly and unexpectedly, and we strongly advise you to confirm important details locally before traveling, including information on visas, health and safety, traffic and transport, accommodation, shopping and eating out. We also encourage you to stay alert while traveling and to remain aware of your surroundings. Avoid civil disturbances, and keep a close eye on cameras, purses, wallets and other valuables.

While we have endeavored to ensure that the information contained within this guide is accurate and up-to-date at the time of publication, we make no representations or warranties with respect to the accuracy or completeness of the contents of this work and specifically disclaim all warranties, including without limitation warranties of fitness for a particular purpose. We accept no responsibility or liability for any inaccuracy or errors or omissions, or for any inconvenience, loss, damage, costs or expenses of any nature whatsoever incurred or suffered by anyone as a result of any advice or information contained in this guide.

The inclusion of a company, organization or website in this guide as a service provider and/or potential source of further information does not mean that we endorse them or the information they provide. Be aware that information provided through some websites may be unreliable and can change without notice. Neither the publisher or author shall be liable for any damages arising herefrom.

# Travel Resources at Frommers.com

Frommer's travel resources don't end with this guide. Frommer's website, **www.frommers.com**, has travel information on more than 4,000 destinations. We update features regularly, giving you access to the most current trip-planning information and the best airfare, lodging, and car-rental bargains. You can also listen to podcasts, connect with other Frommers.com members through our active-reader forums, share your travel photos, read blogs from guidebook editors and fellow travelers, and much more.

# Frommer's 100 Best Packing Tips

Do you always travel with no fewer than three bags, no matter how many days you're going to be away from home? Do you always feel like you've brought half your closet, but have nothing to wear? Do you often discover that you've left important items at home?

If you answered yes to any of these questions, you're certainly not alone! Packing for any trip often proves to be a daunting (and sometimes anxiety-inducing) task for many. From what to bring and how to actually pack it, to what to leave home and what to buy at your destination, there are lots of things to take into consideration.

Whether you're an over-packer or an under-packer (while less common than over-packers, they do exist—you know who you are!), the end result is typically the same: You leave behind the items you *really* need. Over-packers pack around the notion that the more stuff they have, the more prepared they will be for any and all situations. But in fact, it's often the opposite! Over-packers tend to throw all sorts of things in their suitcase without any sort of plan, and sometimes they're even unaware of what's actually inside their bags. Plus, the more unnecessary gear they tote, the more likely they are to forget important items.

Under-packers commonly say "Oh, if I don't have it, I'll just buy it there!" While that's definitely something to take into consideration when packing, it's crucial to limit purchases to items that are worth it when it comes to space in your suitcase, money, and time. For example, it's smart to buy full-size bottles of certain toiletries when you reach your destination because doing so will free up space in your suitcase and will prevent you from having to check your bag, which may mean additional fees each leg of your trip. But other items, like hiking shoes, extra memory cards for your camera, or a cell phone charger, may not only be overpriced at your destination, but they may also be hard to find. And the last thing you want to do is waste precious vacation time hunting for a forgotten necessity.

This book will provide you with the know-how to become a savvy packer and start your next vacation stress-free—and with confidence that everything in your suitcase has a purpose. The key is to streamline the process as much as possible. You want to strike a

Previous page: This book will help you pack everything from sweaters to souvenirs like a pro.

Don't let this happen to you!

balance between the amount of stuff that is reasonable for your duration and type of trip, and what you feel you actually need to bring with you. To get started, there are certain tips and rules that you should keep in mind when preparing for any trip type, from family vacations to business trips. The next several pages will provide an overview of the basics that will be covered in further detail throughout the book.

As you're reading, keep in mind that no matter how much knowledge you are equipped with, it is impossible to assemble a well-packed suitcase in the frenzied 5 minutes before you're supposed to leave for the airport. It is imperative to spend time on the packing process. The more thoughtful you are, the more you research, edit, and really think about each and every item that goes into your suitcase, the more smoothly your trip will go, from start to finish.

# Luggage Types

Know the different kinds of bags and suitcases so that you can pick the one that best suits your needs. Here's a breakdown of the types of bags mentioned throughout this book.

**Wheelie bags:** This is a generic term used to identify bags or suitcases that sit upright, have wheels attached, and are rolled by retractable handles. It can refer to bags with two or four wheels, although bags with four wheels are often called spinners (see next term). Wheelie bags are the most popular kind of suitcase used today and generally come in two different styles: soft-sided and hard-sided. Soft-sided bags are typically made of heavy-duty nylon, but they do come in other fabrics like leather and canvas. Hard-sided bags are usually made of lightweight polycarbonate. Wheelie bags come in all different sizes.

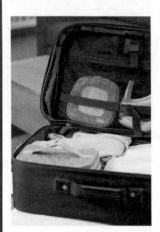

Good organization helps you make the most of your suitcase space.

**Spinner bags:** Like wheelie bags, spinner bags also sit upright and have a retractable handle, but they have four wheels instead of two. The wheels are multidirectional, meaning you can pull and push a spinner in every direction.

**Duffel bags:** Soft-sided and barrel-shaped, duffel bags typically have one or two shoulder straps and zip closed. Traditional duffel bags do not have wheels, but there are plenty of modern versions with wheels attached.

**Weekender bags:** Basically over-size totes or streamlined duffel bags, weekenders are just big enough to hold the essentials needed for a 2- or 3-day trip.

**Rolling garment bags:** Made to hold longer items, such as suits and dresses, rolling garment bags are rectangular in shape and fold in half over themselves. Zippers keep the two halves together and they are rolled by a retractable handle.

**Backpacks:** They are meant to be carried exactly how the name suggests—on your back! There are many different kinds, including those that are meant for everyday use and versions that are used for sports, including hiking, biking, and running. Backpacks for everyday use are basic, top-loading styles with two straps. Sports backpacks include daypacks, hydration packs, waist packs, and extended trip packs (also called expedition or adventure backpacks), and come in all different sizes with a variety of features such as hydration systems and hip belts. You can even find business-oriented, TSA-friendly (Transportation Security Administration) laptop backpacks that zip open and lay flat so you can speed through airport security.

## *General Packing Tips & Tricks*

### The art of packing light

While you're considering what to bring on your trip, prevent yourself from over-packing by checking yourself (every step of the way!) with these three key questions:

1.  **Do I *really* need this?** Be brutally honest with yourself when answering this question! Think about whether or not you can get through your trip without it (especially when it comes to gadgets and their accessories). If you're unsure or hesitant about your answer, you probably don't need it.
2.  **Will I wear this more than once?** If the answer is no, don't bring it. Only bring items you plan on wearing at least twice. You can always hand-wash things if necessary. Both Eucalan (www.eucalan.com) and Soak (www.soakwash.com) offer travel variety packs of their products, which are designed for hand washing and don't even require rinsing. Knitting boutiques are a great place to find these and other similar products for hand washing. (And if you're really in a pinch, you can always use shampoo to wash your clothes.) If you're going on an outdoor adventure trip, consider bringing clothesline as well.

    Pack simple outfits—planning them around a neutral color palette is helpful—so that you can mix-and-match items. Don't bring the patterned shirt that only goes with a single pair of shorts! Sticking to simple outfits will not only help you get more mileage out of your wardrobe, it will also ensure that you will be prepared for all different occasions and settings. A basic little black dress or a collared shirt can instantly be dressed up with a couple of accessories for an unexpected night out.
3.  **Is it better to buy this at my destination?** This is something that separates the savvy packers from the amateurs! Be smart about what you can afford to buy or rent once you've arrived at your destination, especially if bringing the item in question means having to check a bag. For instance, instead of bringing a full bottle of sunscreen, bring just enough in a

small bottle to get you through a couple of days and buy a larger bottle as needed. It will cost less than paying fees both ways to check your bag.

## Maximizing space & minimizing wrinkles

Remember, the more neatly you pack the less space your items will take up and the more you will actually be able to fit in your suitcase. Always pack heavy to light—bulky items like shoes goes on the very bottom, then hefty clothing like jeans and sweaters. Your most delicate items, like lightweight shirts, go on the very top.

While rolling clothes can save space, it can actually *increase* wrinkles. Roll lightweight items that you don't mind getting wrinkled, such as pajamas and gym clothes, and stuff them into crevices—in between pairs of shoes, along the edges of your bag. Stash items like socks and underwear in your shoes.

## Bringing souvenirs home

Don't stuff your suitcase to the max. Allow extra room to accommodate keepsakes from your trip. Even if you don't end up needing all of the space, you will appreciate a lighter bag. At the same time, you want your bag to be relatively full so clothes can't shift around so much they get bunched up and wrinkled. One way to free up souvenir space in your bag is to pack some items that you can toss at the end of your trip if needed, such as small bottles of toiletries or old T-shirts (that you've brought to hike or work out in). Another option is to pack a lightweight reusable bag that will roll or fold up small

Use every bit of space you can— including the space inside your shoes.

# Packing Aids

Packing aids are smart investments, especially if you're a frequent traveler. They're easy to use and can be invaluable in protecting your items, keeping your suitcase organized and your clothing wrinkle-free.

**Packing folders** (or **garment sleeves**) are designed to hold several neatly folded pants, shirts, blouses, sweaters and more in tidy, compact bundles. They come in different sizes and can hold anywhere from 6 to 15 items in one folder. Not only do they aid in reducing wrinkles, but they also help maximize space in your suitcase. Don't worry about being able to fold everything precisely—many come with folding boards to make getting a perfect fold (at the correct size) a cinch. If you know you're not a great folder or you simply dislike doing it, definitely opt for one with a folding board! Typically they're made of durable nylon with Velcro closures. Eagle Creek and Magellan's are go-to brands for these items.

**Packing cubes** also keep your items organized, compact, and in place (instead of shifting around your suitcase, which causes more wrinkles) while you're traveling. They're deeper than folders, hence the name, so they are great for bulkier items. Available in all sorts of sizes, you can fill them with anything from socks and underwear to sweaters and trousers. Usually they zip closed, and you can find versions in see-through materials that allow you to identify what's inside without having to open them. They're also great for keeping damp or soiled items separate from clean clothing. Eagle Creek and Magellan's also make cubes, but other brands to consider include Athalan, Samsonite, Travelon, and Heys.

**Shoe bags** serve two purposes: They keep your footwear from getting dirt on other items in your suitcase, but because you should always pack your shoes in the very bottom of your suitcase, bags also protect your shoes from items that could scuff or scratch them. You can find versions in cotton and synthetic fabrics—both are great options. Most luggage companies make them, and some even include them with certain suitcase models, so it might be something you want to consider when purchasing your next set of luggage.

**Lingerie bags** protect delicate items from snags and tears. Available in all different fabrics and patterns, from basic to fancy, there are plenty of options from which to choose. If you already launder your delicate items in bags specially made to protect them (you can easily find them in stores like Target and Bed Bath & Beyond), you can use those for travel, too. And when you return home just pop them right in the washing machine!

**Plastic bags** are your number-one defense when guarding your clothes against wrinkles. Use the bags you get from the dry cleaners for larger items and try zip-top bags for smaller pieces. Carefully fold delicate items and place them in individual plastic bags. These go on the very top of your suitcase. The plastic will help reduce friction (which will in turn reduce wrinkles). Plastic bags are also great for organizing accessories and toiletries.

and plan to carry it on the plane on the way home. They also can come in handy if you pick up something that's too bulky or awkward to pack in your suitcase. If you're traveling by car, definitely throw some reusable bags in the trunk to accommodate any extras you pick up, and be sure to leave some extra space for them.

## Traveling overseas

When packing for an international trip, in addition to figuring out if you need both an adapter and a converter and making sure that your passport and necessary visas are squared away, it's important to familiarize yourself with cultural norms. It's often easier (and safer!) to move through a country when you dress according to the norms, especially if you're a woman and especially if you're traveling alone. Also, you may be required to dress a certain way to enter certain buildings such as churches, mosques, and temples around the world. Bare arms and legs are often prohibited.

# *Air Travel*

## Getting through security

Savvy packers don't get held up at security checkpoints. Breeze through quickly and smoothly by keeping the following in mind:

Your liquids must be packed according to TSA's (Transportation Security Administration) 3-1-1 guidelines: Place bottles that hold no more than 3.4 ounces in a quart-size, zip-top plastic bag. Each passenger is allowed one bag and it must be taken out of your luggage and placed in the bin to be X-rayed. Because you'll have to take it out at the checkpoint, don't bury it at the bottom of your suitcase! For easy access, stash it in one of your suitcase's outside pockets, in your purse, or at the very top of your suitcase (when it's standing upright) so that you can unzip one of the zippers and grab it easily. You cannot take bottled drinks through security, so throw them away beforehand. If you have a reusable water bottle, just pour the liquid out before getting in line. Be aware that you're allowed to bring bottles of medications, baby formula and food, and breast milk that exceed 3.4 ounces—just be sure to alert a security officer at the checkpoint.

Familiarize yourself with what you can and cannot take with you, such as specific food items. If you're ever in doubt about a specific item, check it before you leave. TSA's website, www.tsa.gov, has a detailed list of allowed and prohibited items. You can also download their mobile app, My TSA (for free, at the iTunes Store) for use on the go. In addition to information about airport delays and general TSA rules, the "Can I Bring?" tool allows you to type in an item and get information about whether or not it will be allowed through security. It's great for last-minute checks.

Be prepared to remove your coat, shoes, and any items that could set off the metal detector alarm, such as belts, jewelry, and watches. Also be ready to remove everything from your pockets, including your cellphone, wallet, and keys.

Carry your laptop in a sleeve or a TSA-friendly computer bag to prevent having to take your laptop completely out of its carrier at security. Also, keep in mind that tablets and e-readers do not have to be removed from their cases at security.

Pack your bag neatly. The more organized your carry-on, the easier it will be for security officers to clearly see and identify items

Use travel-size bottles for any liquid toiletries you carry on the plane.

# Converters & Adapters

Follow these instructions to make sure your gadgets work while traveling abroad.

**Adapters:** Start by checking the shape of outlets in your destination country. The flat, parallel, two-prong plug system used in the United States is seldom used anywhere else in the world, so if you're going to a different country, chances are the sockets will be shaped differently than your plug. You can find a chart of socket shapes used around the world on sites like electricaloutlet.org and magellans.com.

Once you've determined the proper outlet shape, you'll need to buy a **plug adapter** to make your gadget compatible. An adapter is an attachment that simply changes the shape of a plug so that it will fit into a wall socket that is shaped differently. If you're going to want to charge multiple items at once, you may want to buy a few adapters or bring along an extension cord, power strip, or an outlet multiplier. Adapters vary in size and price, so it's wise to comparison shop. The Internet is a great resource, along with stores like RadioShack, Brookstone, and Best Buy. If you're traveling to Europe, the adapter you will need is small and cheap, especially if you buy it online!

One more tip: Before purchasing your adapter, check to see if any of the electrical items you'll be using has a three-prong plug (with the round "grounding" prong underneath the two flat prongs) instead of the usual two-prong plus. If it does, you'll want to be sure your adapter will accept three prongs. You can use a two-prong plug in an adapter that accepts three prongs, but not vice versa.

**Converters & transformers:** Next, take a look at your actual appliance. There should be a sticker on it indicating whether or not it is dual voltage. If it says "Input: 110–240volts, 50/60Hz" then it is dual voltage and your appliance will work with a simple plug adapter. U.S. appliances run on 110V and appliances in most other countries run on 220–240 volts. (**Side note:** Appliances in different countries also run at different hertz frequencies, either 60Hz or 50Hz—U.S. appliances run at 50Hz—but the thing you need to pay attention to is the voltage.) Most laptop and camera battery chargers are dual voltage, and most newer appliances are dual voltage as well. If you travel often, get into the habit of only buying gadgets that are dual voltage. It will save you time, money, and frustration!

If your appliance is not dual voltage you will need either a converter or a transformer. A converter is needed for items that heat up or have a motor, such as hairdryers, fans, and irons, that you only plan on using for short periods of time. Converters temper excess power, allowing you to plug a lower-voltage device (for example, a U.S. plug that's 110V) into a higher-voltage socket (for example, a European socket that's 220V).

For electronics that do not heat up or that have built-in computer chips (such as an alarm clock), you will need a transformer.

Always make sure that your converter or transformer delivers the watts your appliance needs, especially if you are using something like a high-wattage blow-dryer. It's important to pick the proper connector because using the wrong one can fry your device, cause a power outage, or even electrocute you! So if you're ever in doubt, consult with your product's manufacturer or visit a store where a knowledgeable salesperson can help you figure out what you need. You may want to invest in a global adapter or converter kit—both are equipped to cover you in different countries around the world.

in your bag and the less likely you are to be pulled aside for further screening. Pay special attention to cords for your gadgets—if they're jumbled up they can really distort the X-ray images, so make sure they're neatly coiled.

## Luggage restrictions & considerations

**Carry-on bags:** You're allowed one carry-on and one personal item (laptop bag, camera bag, diaper bag, and so on) on domestic flights. Your carry-on bag must not be more than 22"×14"×9", or 45 linear inches, which is your bag's length + width + height. On some international carriers, particularly budget airlines like easyJet and Ryanair in Europe, your personal item is counted as your one allowed carry-on (and the size and weight limits for carry-on bags can be different than those for U.S. carriers), so you will most likely have to pay to check a bag.

Laptop sleeves can protect your computer and help you get through security quickly and easily.

**Checked bags:** On domestic flights most airlines charge an additional fee for each checked bag (on international flights you're allowed to check one bag for free). If your bag exceeds 50 pounds you will have to pay extra.

**Special equipment:** Many sports items like skis, snowboards, and fishing poles are allowed as your checked baggage. Different weight and size limits apply, so be sure to check your airline's website for detailed information. Strollers are not allowed on board but can be checked either at the check-in counter or at the gate. In order for you to check a stroller at the gate it must be collapsible. It does not count as one of your carry-on bags and will be delivered at the door of the plane after your flight.

FAA (Federal Aviation Administration)-approved car seats are allowed on board, assuming you purchased a seat for your child. If you're traveling with a lap child, you can bring your car seat to the gate in case there's an empty seat on the plane you can use. If not, you can gate-check it. You can also check car seats with your luggage, but keep in mind checked luggage is often handled roughly and the seat could be damaged en route. Also consider that if your seat gets lost en route it's unlikely the airline will be able to provide you with a new one when you arrive at your destination, and you'll be stuck. For those reasons, gate-checking is probably safest. At the time of this writing, airlines were not charging any fees for transporting car seats or strollers.

**Lost or delayed bags:** Prepare for the worst when it comes to checking your bags. Pack as though you're assuming it will be delayed at least a couple of days. Ask yourself what you absolutely cannot live without and pack those items in your carry-on bag. Some of those items may include prescription medications, eye glasses, any additional travel documents you might need, and at least one change of clothing. If you're traveling with another person, you may want to pack a set of clothes in their bag (and vice versa) in case just one of your bags shows up at baggage claim.

Make sure your contact information is somewhere on your bag, either on your own luggage tag or the one provided at the ticket counter. List your cellphone number instead of your home phone number, which won't do you any good because you're not there! Know your bag well enough (color, size, distinguishing marks and tags) so that you can provide an accurate description if your bag is lost. Consider taking a picture of your bag with your phone before you head out, especially if you're traveling as a family with multiple bags.

## *Road Trips*

### Knowing where you're going

Research your route, even if you're using a GPS! Your GPS may malfunction, leaving you without a clue where you're going. So plot out your path ahead of time and bring paper maps as extra backup.

## Preparing for emergencies

Make sure your trunk is stocked with everything you need in case of an emergency, such as a flat tire or a dead battery. This should include everything from a spare tire, a jack, and lug wrench to jumper cables, an umbrella, and a flashlight. Check that all items are in your trunk and that they're in working condition. Never assume that they are—physically inspect and account for each item! The last thing you want to discover on the road is that your spare tire is flat too, or that the batteries in your flashlight are dead.

# Weekend Trips

YOUR GOAL WHEN PACKING FOR 2 OR 3 DAYS SHOULD BE TO TRAVEL as light as possible. "The best way to pack your suitcase is to only bring what you really need," says Ari Goldberg, CEO and co-founder of StyleCaster. "If you go away for three days you only need one pair of jeans, not three!"

It's much easier to travel light when your packing list is well thought out. Waiting until the last minute will only make things harder on yourself. So start thinking about what you're going to take in advance and edit items right up until you leave. Be smart about what you absolutely cannot live without and what you can afford to buy at your destination to lighten your load. Limit yourself to one carry-on and one personal bag (even if you're road-tripping!).

Remember: The less you have to fight with your bags to lug them to your destination, the happier you will be!

TIP

# Try a weekender bag.

Consider a weekender bag if you're truly traveling light. It's basically an over-size tote or streamlined duffel bag specifically designed to only hold what you need for about 2 to 3 days of travel. So it's a great way to force yourself to really pare down what you're taking. It also eliminates the need to roll a suitcase, which may be easier to maneuver in certain situations. Go for one with sturdy arm and shoulder straps (short tote handles and a long, adjustable strap), so that you'll have the option to shift the weight or free up a hand or shoulder when needed. Look for durable nylon, leather, or canvas bags with several inside pockets to keep your items organized. Start with your favorite luggage or handbag brand and check out their selections—you'll likely find one there. Also consider fashion brands like Fossil (for great canvas options with

Previous page: Gazing at giant redwoods in Muir Woods National Monument, California.

Look for a weekender bag with multiple straps and pockets.

handy pockets), LeSportsac, or Kipling (both make colorful options in heavy-duty nylon; Kipling also makes rolling duffels). Since there are so many different options out there, you can really find one that suits your packing needs as well as your personal style.

If you prefer not to carry the weight on your shoulders for whatever reason (maybe you have an injury, or you're carrying an infant), then opt for a wheelie bag. Both hard-sided and soft-sided bags will work, as long as they fit the airlines' carry-on baggage requirements (approximately 22"x14"x9").

For your personal bag, opt for a purse, small messenger bag, or a backpack that can double as your day bag. For such a short trip you should definitely limit yourself to no more than two bags, so if you need to bring your laptop, stow it in a sleeve instead of a separate computer bag. That way you can slip it into either your larger bag or your personal bag.

As a general rule for any trip, always pack the items you will definitely need while on the plane in your personal bag and never in your rolling carry-on. Space can run out in the overhead bins, especially as fees for checked baggage continue to increase, so there is always a possibility you may be forced to surrender your suitcase while boarding. It may be delivered to you plane-side after your flight, but if it's checked all the way to your final destination, it won't be available to you until you pick it up at baggage claim. You don't want to be stuck without something you need, and you also want to avoid having to scramble to yank something out of your bag before handing it over to the flight attendant.

TIP

2

# Limit yourself to one outfit per day.

Bring only one outfit for each day of your trip. To make this doable, choose versatile clothes that can be dressed up or down with accessories. Small extras like jewelry, ties, belts, scarves, and clutches won't take up too much space in your suitcase, but will instantly lend a dressy feel or a pop of color.

Build outfits around a neutral color like black, navy, or khaki so that you can mix-and-match pieces if needed. Stick to solid-col-

Stretch your travel wardrobe by dressing simple, neutral pieces up and down with scarves and other accessories.

ored, unfussy basics like drapey dresses, T-shirts, and black pants to maximize wardrobe flexibility. Choose space-saving fabrics like cotton, cotton blends, rayon, cashmere, and wool blends. Fine gauge knit sweaters are not bulky and travel well. Also, anything with a bit if stretch in it will hold its shape and fold up neatly.

For your travel outfit, "a T-shirt, jeans, and shoes that slip off are fine, a sweater because it's cold on the plane, and sunglasses," says Goldberg. You'll not only stay comfortable, but this will keep what should be your two bulkiest clothing items—a sweater and a pair of jeans—out of your suitcase.

TIP
3

# Try to live with two pairs of shoes.

"I like to keep shoes to a minimum when I travel, so I'll wear a nicer pair like Tod's driving loafers and bring a pair of sandals," says Brandon Perlman, co-founder of StyleCaster. Definitely wear your bulkiest shoes on the plane and pack pairs that can be flattened in cloth shoe bags or plastic bags so they don't get your clothes dirty. Lightweight shoes made of a soft material are amazing to travel with. They won't weigh you down and the more they can be flattened, the less room they will take up in your suitcase. TOMS (www.toms.com) is a great go-to brand for ultra-lightweight canvas shoes (plus, when you buy a pair, TOMS donates a pair to a child in need). Women, if you can go without heels, absolutely leave them home. There are so many stylish flats and sandals that go with everything, even dressy outfits. It will save so much room!

If you can get away with only bringing one pair of shoes, kudos! But two is perfectly reasonable.

TIP
4

# Pack clothes neatly and carefully.

"Don't underestimate the power of folding your clothes neatly— that alone saves so much space!" says Melanie Fascitelli, Founder of Clos-ette and clos-ette too. Start thinking about what you're going to take with you a week in advance. You can wait until the day before you leave to actually pack, but it's best to avoid packing the day of if at all possible. The farther in advance you start preparing, the less likely you are to overpack. Plus, the more organized you can be at the start of your trip, the better you will fare. Also, the more care you take in actually arranging things in your suitcase, the more you will maximize your space. A neatly folded pair of jeans takes up much less room than a pair crumpled up into a ball!

Place heavy items like shoes in the bottom of your bag. If you're taking a wheelie bag, nestle them in between the supports. Stuff socks into shoes to save space. If there is room in between your shoes, roll thin items like tanks and T-shirts and wedge them into the empty crevices. Rolling can save space, but it can also cause more wrinkles, so only roll items that you don't mind getting wrinkled or that don't wrinkle very easily. Layer your heaviest clothing items next, including jeans and sweaters. Place delicate items on the very top in plastic bags if wrinkle-prone (be sure to squeeze out any excess air). "Plastic helps keep your clothes fresh and wrinkle-free without taking up space," says Fascitelli. The plastic bags you get from the dry cleaner are perfect for packing—save them up and reuse them.

TIP

5

# Consolidate your gadgets.

Remember, you're only going on a short trip so be very realistic about what you need to take. Bring only what you absolutely cannot live without. If you're nervous about having to check in at work while you're gone, call ahead to see if your hotel has a business center before adding your laptop on your packing list. Since you're only going for such a short period of time, consider taking advantage of your time away and unplugging for a few days! E-readers and tablets are better options than laptops and thick paperbacks. Always bring the proper chargers, but stick to one of each type. For instance, if two of your gadgets require a micro USB cord to charge, such as a Blackberry or a Kindle, only bring one of the cords and use it to charge both. But always test them at home before you leave to make sure the cord does indeed charge both devices.

If you're traveling overseas pack the proper adapter or converter when needed (see the Business Trips chapter for more information on international gadgets and converters).

TIP
6

# Downsize your extras.

Bring compact, travel-friendly sizes of as many as items as possible. This includes blow-dryers, flatirons, electric shavers, toothbrushes, and toiletries. Consider buying a set of toiletries with bottles all 3.4 fluid ounces or less in a quart-size zippered plastic bag. You can buy them either with product already inside, or you can fill your own. No need to bring along a fancy toiletry bag—all of your toiletries should fit inside the allowed quart-size plastic bag. Even if you're traveling by car, restrict yourself to these limits. You don't want your liquids to weigh you down! Flight001 makes great sets of empty bottles, and www.3floz.com is a gold mine for pre-filled sets for men, women, and children.

Keep in mind that the change in pressure during the flight can cause liquids to expand and overflow, which may cause your bottles to explode. Prevent this by making sure none of your bottles are filled up to the very top—either use a small portion of pre-filled bottles before you leave or leave a little room at the top when filling your own. Leaving a little room to accommodate expansion will help keep the caps firmly in place.

Whenever possible, replace your liquids with items that don't have to go in your quart-size bag. For instance, instead of a bottle of liquid face cleanser, opt for cleansing towelettes. All of the major beauty brands make them—Ponds, Biore, L'Oreal. Go beyond your basic cleanser with towelette versions of everything from hand sanitizer and lotion to eyeglass cleaner. La Fresh (www.lafresh group.com) makes those items and more in towelette form. If your can't find an item in a towelette or you're loyal to a specific brand or product, try saturating cotton balls or cotton rounds with the solution (like astringent or toner). Soak enough cotton balls to last you through the weekend (one cotton ball per use), place them in a plastic zip-top bag, and squeeze the air out before sealing. It will help keep the bag from opening accidentally and it will also make the bag more compact. This is a tremendous space-saver, and the bag won't count as one of your liquids.

If you travel frequently, especially on short trips, get into the habit of collecting travel-size bottles of items wherever you go. When you're out shopping, always ask for samples of your favorite products, including lotion, facial cleansers, perfumes, and hair styling products. Department store beauty counters are loaded with travel-size samples—even when it comes to high end products—and most of the time all you have to do is ask for them. Even when you're shopping online, many websites offer free samples with purchase, so take this into consideration when you troll the web for your next toiletry or cosmetic purchase. Also, when you stay at a hotel, never leave unopened toiletries behind. If you can squeeze them into your bag, take them—they will come in handy on your next trip.

Consolidate any medications you need to take, too. Instead of bringing several separate bottles, take out only the pills you will need for the weekend and stash them in a pill case. Choose the smallest one that you can get away with.

## Packing List

- ☐ Neutral-colored clothing
- ☐ Dressy accessories
- ☐ Flat shoes
- ☐ Camera
- ☐ Toiletry set (with small bottles)

# Business Trips

BUSINESS TRIPS OFFER THEIR OWN SET OF PACKING CHALLENGES. You want to arrive put-together and prepared, and to achieve that you'll need to start planning your packing the moment you start planning your trip. Be meticulous when mapping out your itinerary so that you are as prepared as possible for each meeting and social outing. Don't get bogged down with preparing for the unexpected. If you are completely covered for what is expected, you will be able to make your existing wardrobe and accessories work for the unexpected, too!

If your work takes you to far-flung locales, make sure you are well versed in the customs, etiquette, plug sizes, and electrical currents in your destination country. It's also a good idea to be aware of baggage allowances of local airlines. All of that information will prove invaluable.

TIP

7

# Invest in a quality suitcase.

It's worth buying a set of top-notch bags for business travel, particularly when it comes to your carry-on and especially if you travel often for work. Quality luggage will look more professional and will also last longer than cheaper versions, which will save you money in the long run. Companies like Travelpro (a favorite of airline pilots and flight attendants), Samsonite, and Briggs & Riley set the standard for wheelie bags.

Look for well-made bags with sturdy zippers and multiple pockets and compartments to accommodate your stuff. Expandable styles will give you more flexibility. Go beyond basic black and opt for a suitcase in a different color, especially if it's a bag you're checking! Rich, muted colors like tan, gray, dark green, and blue stand out on the luggage carousel but are still professional. If you prefer basic black or you already own a set in that color, attach a can't-miss luggage tag to the handle to make your bag easily

Previous page: New York's bustling Grand Central Station.

identifiable. Rather than filling out the card with your home address, tuck your business card inside the slot instead. You can also tie a brightly colored ribbon to the handle to make your bag stand out, but a luggage tag is the better option for more conservative settings.

If you're traveling with a laptop, you may want to consider a carry-on suitcase with a dedicated laptop compartment. This will eliminate the need to carry a separate computer bag and will also free up space in your personal bag. Another option is to place your laptop in a sleeve and slip it into one of your suitcase's outside pockets. It makes for easy access, and if you plan to use your computer during the flight you can take it out before you place your bag in the overhead bin.

When traveling overseas, be aware that baggage allowances and requirements may be different. While most domestic carriers allow your carry-on suitcase to stand 22 inches high, many international airlines only allow bags up to 20 inches tall. Also keep in mind that when flying on a budget airline, such as Ryanair or easyJet in Europe, purses and laptop bags actually count as your one allowed carry-on. This means you're likely to have to check your bag and if it's more than 20 kg (which is 44 lb., vs. the domestic weight limit of 50 lb.) you will have to pay extra fees. In these situations it truly pays to travel light!

For added peace of mind, consider attaching a TSA-approved lock to any checked luggage. Security officers have master keys for these approved locks so that they can be opened it needed. If your lock is not TSA-approved, then it may be cut off if your bag needs to be opened. Companies like Safe Skies and Travel Sentry make approved locks. Visit www.tsa.gov for more information.

TIP

8

# Get a TSA-friendly laptop bag.

If you prefer to travel with a separate laptop bag, look for one that's TSA-friendly so that you don't have to remove your computer at the security checkpoint. Most manufacturers now make bags and sleeves that fit the following TSA standards:

- Has a designated laptop-only section
- The laptop-only section completely unfolds to lie flat on the X-ray belt
- No metal snaps, zippers, or buckles inside, underneath, or on top of the laptop-only section
- No pockets on the inside or outside of the laptop-only section
- Nothing is packed in the laptop-only section other than the computer itself

Sleeves, tri-fold bags, and what the TSA calls "butterfly styles" (with a middle zipper that unzips and allows both sides of the bag to lie completely flat; visit tsa.gov for illustrations) are all approved and will keep you from having to take your laptop out of the bag. Look for a bag that follows these guidelines and you'll zip through security! Many companies specifically call out bags that are checkpoint-friendly to make picking one a cinch.

Don't forget to look for a sturdy, comfortable shoulder strap, especially if your computer is weighty, as company-issued laptops tend to be. Extra padding is a must! Also choose one that attaches comfortably to your suitcase—a strap that slips over the handle is great and easy to use on-the-go. Separate compartments for cords, chargers, and files are very handy to have.

***Note:*** Tablets do not have to be removed from your bag (neither do e-readers), so if you can get by with just an iPad, leave the laptop at home. If you need to do more extensive typing than you are comfortable doing on a tablet, consider a Bluetooth keyboard. Brands like Verbatim make compact, travel-friendly styles that fold in half when not in use. It may turn out to be a lifesaver and is still less bulky than a laptop.

You also may want to consider investing in a super-lightweight laptop such as a MacBook Air if you travel extensively with your laptop.

TIP

9

# Dress to impress.

When boarding the plane "you should dress like you never know who you're going to meet along the way," says Ari Goldberg, CEO and co-founder of StyleCaster. Even if you don't have to go straight to the office or a meeting as soon as you land, "traveling is a great networking opportunity." And if you have to hit the ground running, you'll definitely want to arrive looking professional and polished! When in doubt, it's always better to be overdressed than underdressed. You can always remove a tie, undo a top button, or push back sleeves for a more relaxed look if you feel overdressed. If you're traveling overseas, check to make sure you don't break any attire-related traditions or customs. A clothing faux pas is an easy way to make a bad first impression, so do your research ahead of time.

"Bring at least two suits and wear one on the plane," says Brandon Perlman, co-founder of StyleCaster. "Don't travel with a tie on. Instead, put it on right before you arrive so that you're as comfortable as possible." Choose two suits that complement each other so that you can mix-and-match separates to get more mileage out of them. Black is always good to bring, as are gray and navy.

Look for dress shirts made of wrinkle-resistant fabrics—Brooks Brothers is a great go-to brand. If you can get away with a different color, avoid wearing a white shirt while traveling because it shows dirt too easily. Instead, opt for a color like blue or a subtle striped pattern that will help hide dirt and spills. It's a good idea to bring along an instant stain remover like Tide To Go or Dryel On The Go. They're compact and prefilled with cleaning solution to get rid of stains on the fly.

Women have more wiggle room when it comes to shirt options. Instead of a button-up shirt, layer a top that's more relaxed, such as a blouse or camisole, underneath a blazer. Stick to a polished version without too many embellishments in a dark color that will hide dirt and stains. If you don't have to wear a suit, a dress is also a great option for the plane. You may find it more comfortable (and easier to keep wrinkle-free than separates!) and there are plenty of stylish yet comfortable options.

As for suit pants, skirts, and blazers, stick to wrinkle-resistant fabrics, classic styles, and colors and patterns that go with everything. Wool and wool blends really hold up well. A lightweight blend like gabardine can be worn year-round, even in summer. Cotton twill is another great option. Always avoid silk and linen, as they wrinkle easily.

Wear your suit jacket on the plane, or if it's too hot, carry it over your arm. If you don't want to keep it with you at your seat, ask a flight attendant if there's a closet where it can be stowed; oftentimes it's not a problem.

TIP

**10**

# Avoid a separate garment bag.

Plastic bags can help keep delicate items wrinkle-free.

Don't carry your business attire in a separate garment bag. They are bulky and awkward to carry, especially with another bag in tow. Instead, pack all of your clothes in your suitcase. If you prefer the functionality of a garment bag, go for a sturdy rolling garment bag.

Pack your bag from heavy to light, with shoes in dust bags on the bottom and delicate items, like suits, on the very top. Place wrinkle-prone items neatly folded in separate plastic bags. "I make sure items are neatly and tightly folded so that they don't shift in my suitcase," says Goldberg. This will definitely cut down on wrinkles.

Place heavy, bulky items at the bottom of your bag, and lay delicate, wrinkle-prone items on top.

Wherever you're staying, call ahead to see what dry cleaning and pressing services are available to you. "I don't worry about wrinkles too much, I either get my business attire pressed at the hotel or I find a dry cleaner nearby and just get it steamed," says Perlman. "Lots of hotels offer complimentary pressing, but ask first because if they do charge it can be expensive!"

If you're traveling to a remote location or you are unsure of the services that will be available to you, consider a hand-held travel steamer. That way you won't have to worry about it, and they're great for quickly getting rid of wrinkles. Brands like Jiggy make great travel steamers. A wrinkle-release spray is another option worth considering. It's easy to use—just spritz it onto your clothing, tug the fabric slightly, and smooth it with your hand. Spray releasers work better on cotton-based fabrics, so be sure to read the labels carefully. Brands like Downy make sprays in travel-friendly sizes.

TIP

11

# Wear comfy shoes.

You don't have to sacrifice your feet in order to stay polished. There are plenty of options and backup pairs that will help you arrive with your feet intact.

Men should wear lace-free dress shoes or "slip-on loafers for easy on, easy off" while traveling, says Perlman. Scour your closet or go shopping to find your most comfortable pair. If you know a certain pair causes blisters, don't wear them, no matter how much you like the way they look! Cole Haan makes pairs with Nike Air cushioning for an extra-comfy fit—and they even make heels for women with the same sneaker technology! Tod's also makes comfortable options. A quality pair of thick socks can also go along way in preventing blisters.

Women, unless you're particularly adroit at walking in heels, don't wear them to the airport. They may hurt your feet and will definitely slow you down if you have to run to catch your flight! Stick to a comfortable pair of refined flats—black always works. If you do have to go straight to a meeting when you arrive and you must wear heels, pack them in your carry-on and change them when you arrive. Place them on top so that you're not digging through your suitcase when you're in a hurry. Tod's, Cole Haan, and Geox all make classic, comfortable pumps that are suitable for any occasion.

Depending on how long you're traveling, you may want to bring an extra pair of dress shoes, but don't forget about a pair of shoes for leisure time as well. Even if it's just walking around the hotel, it's always good to give your feet a break! Women, simple flats are good options, and men, go with what's comfortable, whether it's a loafer or driving shoe. Avoid pairs that are dirty or on their last legs. ***Rule of thumb:*** If you would be embarrassed to be seen in them if you ran into a colleague, then don't bring them at all! Even your leisure shoes should be polished enough to work in most settings.

TIP

**12**

# Keep track of your tech.

It's especially important to keep your gadgets organized when traveling for business. The more organized you are, the easier it will be for you to find things when you need them and the less likely you are to lose a vital piece of equipment. Make a list of everything you will need to take with you ahead of time, including files (digital and hard copies). As you're packing, lay everything out in front of you so that you can see everything clearly. Mark them off the list as you place each item in your bag.

If you're checking a bag, pack all of your gadgets, along with any chargers and accessories that go with them, in your carry-on. Never pack a device in a bag separate from its charger! They are

Keep all your cords and chargers organized in one place.

useless without each other. You can, however, pack them in the same bag but in different sections or compartments. It's often easier to keep all of the chargers and accessories together, either in a specific carrying case (camera cases or makeup bags both work surprisingly well for this; of course a zip-top bag works, too) or strapped into something like an organizer from Cocoon (www.cocooninnovations.com). They make clever organizers (called Grid-It!) with lots of rubberized elastic straps to keep all of your gadgets and their accessories in place. There are many different sizes and versions, including options with built-in sleeves for your tablet and styles specifically made for travel.

Utilize all of your suitcase's extra pockets inside and out to help keep you organized. This goes for laptop bags, too. Protect files with plastic sleeves or folders so they don't get damaged en route.

TIP

13

# Stay plugged in overseas.

When traveling abroad, make sure you have the proper gear to charge your electronics. Do your research and bring the proper adapter. Adapters don't change the electrical current, they simply

---

## Cellphones

International roaming charges can cost an arm and a leg! So if you're going to need to use your phone while you're there you might want to consider buying a cheap phone that's unlocked to work on any network, or a local SIM card when you arrive. Both will allow you to utilize cell networks in your destination country, which will mean cheaper rate options.

---

attach to your existing plug and change the shape so that it fits into that country's wall socket. You only need an adapter if your item is either dual voltage (check the actual appliance—it will indicate whether or not it is dual voltage; most laptop and camera battery chargers are) or if you're traveling to a country that uses the same 100–125 volt system as North America. If you're traveling to a country that uses 220–240 volts (which is typical in Europe) and your gadget is not dual voltage, you will need to bring a converter in addition to an adapter.

Converters and transformers actually convert the electrical current. Keep in mind that the proper one is needed for electric shavers, flatirons, and blow-dryers. It can be confusing, but do your due diligence—you can risk blowing fuses, permanently damaging your appliance, and sometimes even starting a fire if you do not have the proper devices. If you're unsure, head to a store like RadioShack, Best Buy, or Brookstone and ask for help. Magellan's has a great interactive tool on their website (www.magellans.com) that takes the guesswork out of finding the correct one.

For more information, see the box "Converters & Adapters" in the introduction to this book.

TIP
14

# Arm yourself with backups.

If it's crucial that you stay connected while on your trip, be sure to arm yourself with backup power. Check out backup cellphone chargers or battery extenders to give your gadgets a boost on the go. Philips and Powermat (www.powermat.com) both make good options. Brands like Mophie (www.mophie.com) make iPhone cases with built-in rechargeable batteries. These types of cases can be a tad bulky, but may be worth having on hand.

If you're heading overseas, bring an extension cord or a power multiplier so that you only need one adapter to charge several gadgets at once. They're also useful if there are a limited number of available outlets.

Hardcopies are the best backups to digital files, but at the very least make sure your files are accessible from another computer in case yours is damaged or lost. E-mail them to yourself or save them somewhere like Google Docs. If you are using Google Docs, don't forget to save all of your documents to your desktop before leaving home. That way you will have access to them without a wireless connection—essential if you plan on doing work while on the plane.

TIP

15

# Keep a prepacked toiletry bag.

If you're a frequent business traveler, consider keeping a set of toiletries that fit the TSA carry-on requirements ready to go at all times. Store it in your bathroom and use it solely for travel on these types of trips. When the bottles get low, refill them with your own products or buy small prefilled bottles. In addition to your liquids, keep it stocked with items like a razor, toothbrush, toothpaste, Q-tips, cotton balls, tweezers, and any other items you use regularly. It will be one less thing you have to worry about when packing.

Also, if your job requires you to travel back and forth to the same location regularly (for example, if you're a consultant and a long-term project requires you to travel to the same city each week), plan to stay at the same hotel each time you make the trip. Not only will it help create a sense of having a home away from home, you can also ask the front desk to hold on to your toiletry bag each time you check out. That way you won't have to deal with hauling your liquids with you each week. Just keep an eye on them and refill bottles when necessary, either back home or at your destination.

*TIP*

**16**

# Check your passport.

Before you head overseas always double check the expiration date on your passport. Even if you think it's valid, check it again so there are no last minute surprises. Keep in mind that some countries require your passport to be valid 3 months after your arrival date—even if you are only staying in that country for a short period of time.

Always carry a photocopy of the first page of your passport (the page with your photo). It will be helpful if you have to apply for a replacement while overseas. In addition to the hardcopy, scan the first page into your computer and e-mail it to yourself. Don't just save it to your laptop, even if you're bringing it with you on your trip. If your computer is lost, damaged, or stolen, you will still have access to the copy if it's in your e-mail.

Also make sure that you have all of the proper vaccinations and visas prior to your trip. For information on vaccinations, visit the CDC's (Centers for Disease Control and Prevention) website, www. cdc.gov. Traveling to several different countries on the same trip? You may want to consult a doctor to make absolutely sure you're covered. Check with the embassy of your destination country for visa requirements. Remember to do both of these well in advance of your travel date!

## Packing List

☐ Suit(s)
☐ Laptop
☐ Cellphone
☐ Adapter/converter
☐ Passport
☐ Photocopy of passport

# Business & Leisure Trips

TACKING ON EXTRA TIME TO EXPLORE WHERE YOU'VE TRAVELED FOR work, whether it's solo or with family members or friends, is a wonderful way to maximize your time and stretch your finances. So it's great to do whenever possible. Once you've gotten your business attire and gear squared away (see the previous chapter), focus your full attention to the leisure part of your trip, including clothing and any accessories and items that you will need (and want!) to have on hand during your free time.

TIP

**17**

# Pick the proper day bag.

Don't forget to pack a day bag to use when you're off the clock. Previous page: Big Ben, in London.

Don't forget to bring a day bag to use during the leisure portion of your trip! Choose one based on your destination and the types of activities you will be participating in once you've broken off from your clients or colleagues. Do you plan on extending your stay in a city so that you can take your time to explore? Consider a tote or a messenger bag. Have an adventure leg of your trip planned? Bring a backpack that's fitted properly for your body. If possible, try to pick a bag you wouldn't mind your colleagues seeing you carry. That way you can use it as your personal item and carry it throughout your trip. Otherwise, pack it in the bottom of your suitcase and keep it there until you split off on your own.

TIP
18

# Keep expenses separate.

When it comes to credit cards, receipts, and money, be sure to keep the items you're using for business-related expenses separate from your personal items. Don't plan to organize things later—you will create more stress and hassle for yourself in the long run. Instead, separate receipts as you go. A smart and easy way to do this is to carry a wallet that's divided into multiple sections. Look for one with two zippered pockets for coins, and ample card slots and compartments for paper bills and receipts. To keep yourself from mixing up the two sides, place cards that are clearly identifiable as business-related in a prominent position on one side, and do the same with cards on the personal side of the wallet. You can also slide a brightly colored paper clip into a card slot on one side

A multisectioned wallet will help you keep personal and business funds separate.

(perhaps the personal side, since the leisure portion of your trip is the one associated with fun!).

If you're headed overseas to a country that uses a lot of coins for currency, such as European countries on the euro, bring a coin pouch. It will be extremely useful in keeping track of your coins. You may want to consider bringing two pouches—one for business and one for leisure. Or stash your business coins in your main wallet and your leisure coins in the pouch.

TIP
19

# Switch up your business attire.

Instead of bringing a completely separate wardrobe for the leisure portion of your trip, build your leisure outfits around your work clothes. For example, "wear a dress shirt with a pair of shorts or jeans," says Kirshan Murphy, style advisor and founder of Theprofessionalgent.com. "An easy way to make it more casual but still keep it stylish is to roll up the sleeves to either just below or above the elbow. You can make it even more casual by unbuttoning a couple of buttons, keeping the lapels untucked, or wearing it open over a tank or T-shirt."

*Men:* If you can get away with it, definitely bring a navy suit. "Every man should have one in his wardrobe," says Murphy. "It is the most versatile and can be easily dressed down. Wear the blazer as a light jacket and pair it with jeans or khakis. Try the pants with a polo shirt." Pullover sweaters, cardigans, and sweater vests all pair well with jeans, too. Pick your dress shoes based on which ones are easily dressed down, such as "brown or black wingtips—they are dressy enough to wear with your suit, but also pair well with khakis," says Murphy.

*Women:* Mix and match the pieces from your suit as well. If possible, avoid a suit with a skirt. Pants are easier to dress down for your leisure attire, and usually more comfortable as well. Instead of a skirt opt for a dress in a fabric like jersey, which doesn't wrinkle easily and can be dressed up or down. Make a dress more casual by changing your shoes and other accessories.

For both men and women, choose additional pairs of shoes to bring according to what you will be doing on the leisure portion of your trip, such as sneakers, water shoes, or sandals. As a general rule, if there is a chance you may run into your colleagues during your down time, do keep this in mind when choosing your clothing. "Being comfortable doesn't mean being sloppy!" says Murphy. So if this is a possibility, it's best to leave your rattiest clothing home and in general stick to items that are casual yet stylish.

TIP
20

# Choose fun extras.

In addition to all of your gadgets for work, bring along leisure tech items, too. Make a list of these items ahead of time to make sure you don't forget them. Run down the list of items you typically

Don't forget to bring the fun stuff, such as personal reading materials, guidebooks, and a camera.

bring on your vacations and build your packing list from there. Bring something to read (either an e-reader or other reading material), along with your camera. If you're already overloaded, leave your SLR camera at home and bring a point-and-shoot model instead. Depending on what you have planned, you may want to bring items like a guidebook, sunscreen, and binoculars.

## Packing List

- ☐ Day bag
- ☐ Two-sided wallet
- ☐ Casual clothing
- ☐ Camera
- ☐ Guidebook

# Family Vacations

Sᴛᴀʏɪɴɢ ᴏʀɢᴀɴɪᴢᴇᴅ ᴀɴᴅ ʙᴇɪɴɢ ᴘʀᴇᴘᴀʀᴇᴅ ғᴏʀ ᴛʜᴇ ᴜɴᴇxᴘᴇᴄᴛᴇᴅ ɪꜱ ᴋᴇʏ when traveling as a family unit, especially when small children are involved. Knowing that you've covered all of your bases will help you to actually *enjoy* the trip, and not feel like you need a vacation from your vacation once you've returned. Make it a group effort, and have each family member pitch in with the prep. "I think when you say to your kids, 'It's each of our responsibility to help out so that we have a nice, smooth trip,' it goes a long way," says Elizabeth Thorp, founder of Poshbrood.com.

TIP
**21**

# Recruit your kids to help you pack.

If they're old enough to do so, involve your kids in gathering their stuff for the trip. Not only will it shorten your to-do list, but it also will help to make sure their favorite snack or toy is not forgotten! "Kids do have things they definitely want to bring," says Thorp. "I let my kids pack their own small bag to take with them on the plane or in the car. I tell them they're in charge of bringing anything they'll want to use on the way—books, dolls, Pillow Pets, art supplies." Just make it clear to them that they will be responsible for handling their own bag throughout the entire trip. "Otherwise they'll pack it with 200 pounds of Barbies and you'll be stuck with another bag!" says Elizabeth.

Kid-size wheelie bags and backpacks are easy for children to manage. Consider fun, brightly colored bags from brands like Trunki, Lands' End, and Heys.

Previous page: Families enjoying a ride at Storyland, in New Hampshire.

Packing cubes can help separate multiple family members' clothes inside the same suitcase.

Pack the rest of their gear, including clothes and toiletries, in a larger suitcase. If you can get away with packing their things in your suitcase, go for it—it's always best to consolidate as much as possible. But if your bag is already full, or if you're traveling with more than one child, designate a separate suitcase just for kids' stuff. Keep things organized by child or by type of item (tops, bottoms, onesies, socks, underwear, toiletries). Ziploc bags or packing cubes from brands like L.L.Bean, Eagle Creek, and Travelon make this a cinch.

When deciding what clothes to pack for small children, it's best to bring enough clothes to last the entire trip. Hand-washing children's clothing can be tedious (especially when trying to clean items that are totally soiled), so save your patience and materials for hand-washing your own clothing when needed. Unlike packing for yourself, don't plan to have your children rewear items once or twice before washing. Their clothes will most likely be too dirty to do that. Instead, just pack enough clothing to get each kid through the entire trip. If you're going on an extended trip, you may want to look into laundry services, but if you're going on typical vacation, say a week or shorter, bring at least one outfit for each kid per day. Then if you end up needing extra, you can hand-wash them or have them laundered. If you're traveling with young children (especially babies), you may want to consider bringing two outfits per day. Always have plenty of plastic bags on hand for storing really dirty items that smell or have gunk on them.

TIP
22

# Put extra clothes within reach.

"I always keep a change of clothes for each kid in my carry-on," says Thorp. "Even if it's an older kid, someone inevitably spills something on themselves and then they're miserable." Pack the outfits in your bag that goes in the overhead bin so they don't take up space in the bag at your feet. Just be sure to place them on the very top so you can grab them easily when needed. If you're traveling with babies or toddlers you may want to pack an extra outfit for yourself as well—you don't want to spend your day wearing the results of an unexpected diaper blowout!

For your second bag, choose a large tote with plenty of pockets inside and out so that everything has a place. Make sure that it will fit easily underneath your seat on the plane or on the floor in the car. Pack it with any items you will need access to throughout the flight, including first aid items, snacks, and extra toys.

As a general rule, if you're checking luggage, it's always a good idea to pack your carry-on bags with at least 2 days' worth of clothes for each family member. This way you're covered if your luggage is lost or delayed.

TIP
23

# Be prepared for cuts, scrapes & spills.

Always bring a fully stocked first-aid kit and put it in your purse or carry-on so that it's with you at all times. Pack everything in something that's clear and waterproof, such as a Ziploc bag or a

# Getting Through Airport Security

Flying with an infant? Don't worry about having to limit the amounts of baby food, formula, and breast milk in your carry-on—all of these items are exempt from the TSA's 3-1-1 rules. Just follow these steps to breeze through security checkpoints on your next trip:

- Pack your baby food, formula, and breast milk separately from the rest of your liquids.
- Tell a security officer at the checkpoint that you're traveling with these items.
- Once you've reached the front of the security line, point these items out to the X-ray operators.

Be aware that breast milk now falls under the same category as liquid medications, so you are permitted to request that the milk does not go through the X-ray machine and instead be visually inspected. Just remember to do this *before* your screening process begins. If you wait until after

Tupperware container. You can make one yourself or buy one already assembled. AAA, Johnson & Johnson, and the American Red Cross all make great first-aid kits in packable sizes, and ME4KIDZ (www.me4kidz.com) makes kits especially for kids.

A basic first-aid kit can include

- Adhesive bandages (in all different shapes and sizes)
- Antiseptic wipes
- Antibiotic ointment
- Thermometer
- Sterile gauze pads
- Medical tape
- Acetaminophen, ibuprofen, and an antihistamine
- Hydrocortisone cream

the process has started the items are required to be sent through the X-ray. Under the same rules, you are allowed to bring frozen breast milk with you as well.

According to the TSA, you may be asked to open one of the containers at the checkpoint, but you will not be asked to taste anything and you will not be asked to feed anything to your child. Keep in mind that even if you are not flying with your child you are still allowed to carry breast milk with you through security.

The TSA has not set a limit as to how much you are allowed to bring with you—the rule is just that "reasonable quantities" are allowed. If you are traveling with your child, at the very least bring enough supplies to get you through until you reach your final destination, plus some extra in case you are delayed in any way.

Also keep in mind that gel or liquid-filled teethers and juice for your baby are also exempt from the 3-1-1 rules.

- Gloves
- Small scissors
- Insect repellent

This list is not all-inclusive—be sure to also include any items that are specific to your location or to the needs of your family. Additional items may include water sterilization tablets, motion sickness medication, prescription medications, or any other over-the-counter medications your family typically uses.

Stash plastic grocery bags (for trash and other messes), hand sanitizer, and moist towelettes like Handi Wipes in the outside pockets of your personal bag for easy access.

In case of more serious emergencies, compile your family's important medical information and have it somewhere that's readily accessible. Whether you e-mail it to yourself or download it to your Kindle or laptop, just make sure each family member knows where to find everything. It's also always a good idea to print out a hard copy and keep it with the rest of your family's travel documents. List the names of prescription medications (along with dosage information for each), allergies, immunization records, and dates of major surgeries. Also include the names and phone numbers of family physicians.

TIP
24

# Bring an arsenal of toys and games.

Don't forget to pack plenty of toys and games to keep kids entertained during your trip.

The best strategy for traveling with kids it to distract, distract, distract! The more you can preoccupy them and make the time pass more quickly (especially on long-haul flights or car rides), the better. If you're traveling with multiple children, be sure you have enough items to go around to avoid squabbles. "Bring small packages of crayons, fresh coloring books, and pads of paper," says Thorp. Also pack their favorite toys, pillows, and blankets, especially if you're traveling by car, where you have more room.

"One trick is to wrap up old, forgotten toys and surprise your kids with them along the way. I get small toys and books they haven't used in a long time from the bottom of the bins in the playroom—or even old Happy Meal toys from the junk drawer—and I wrap them in wrapping paper and keep them in my bag," says Thorp. "This works especially well on road trips when they're stuck in the car for long periods of time. It'll suck up at the very least, 30 minutes of time! It's the presentation, being able to unwrap something. They're so excited to get these little gifts. I do it for every single trip we go on, and they've never gotten tired of it." Dollar stores are another great source for cheap surprise gifts.

Gadgets are also great distractions. "I will surrender every device in the name of peace! Especially when the kids aren't getting along so well, electronics allow them to do something by themselves for a while, which can help," says Thorp. So whatever devices your kids like to play with, bring them! An iPad, Nintendo DS, and portable DVD player are all kid- and travel-friendly. "We'll even let our kids play with my husband's iPhone in a pinch," says Thorp. "There are a lot of great apps for kids out now. Not only Angry Birds, but there are a lot of educational apps too."

Just be sure to complete any downloads, including movies, apps, and music before you leave the house (the night before is best, especially if you're downloading movies). Whether you pay to connect to a wireless network at the airport or you find a free one while on the road, oftentimes the signals aren't strong enough to handle large files. They'll either take hours to download or they won't download at all.

Another rule of thumb: Never give all your toys, games, gadgets, and art supplies to your kids at the start of the trip. "You don't want to come out of the gate full guns blazing with the movies, the iPad, the toys," says Thorp. You want to have some things leftover for the middle and end of the trip, so hold out for as long as you can. You can turn this into a game for your kids. For example on road trips, "say okay, we have to get to this state before you can watch a movie," says Thorp. Then your kids will look forward to their reward for making it through a certain number of hours.

Always consider the noise level and your own patience level when deciding what toys and games to bring with you on your trip. Leave anything home that creates a racket or that you find annoying or headache-inducing. Even if you only find a specific toy mildly irritating at home, remember that you could be stuck with your child playing with that toy for hours on end in confined spaces. So bring toys that will keep the peace for your family and others nearby.

Also avoid toys with lots of different pieces and detachable accessories. You don't want to have to worry about keeping track of a million different pieces (or hunting for them if they are lost). Plus, losing track of precious accessories could be upsetting to your child, and the last thing you need is a temper tantrum. Whenever possible, bring toys and games that aren't super bulky or oversized. Anything that can be packed relatively flat is perfect for traveling. Inflatable toys are especially travel-friendly—they're soft and can be stashed anywhere.

If you're traveling with more than one kid and have lots of toys in tow, you might want to bring along a bag to keep toys and games organized while at your destination. Pack a collapsible mesh storage (one that folds flat) or laundry bag in your suitcase and set it up in your hotel or cruise cabin. It will help cut down on the clutter and keep all your kids' toys in one place.

TIP

25

# Have plenty of snacks on hand.

"A hungry kid is a cranky kid, so snacks are key when you're traveling with kids!" says Thorp. Especially when you're flying, and you have less control over when you get your food and the kind of food you get. Even if certain meals are provided or there is food for purchase, it can take flight attendants a while to reach you. So bringing your own snacks wherever you go is a must!

"In addition to letting them pack their own toys, I also put my kids in charge of packing their own snacks," says Thorp. "I take them into the kitchen and have everything laid out—crackers, granola bars, peanuts, raisins. Then they pick what they want to put in

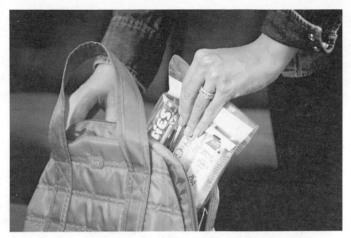

Snacks and drinks can be lifesavers during a long trip.

their carry-on or bag for the car." Of course it's always a good idea to bring extra!

Opt for foods that aren't super messy, and whenever possible go for individually packaged items. Wash fruits and vegetables ahead of time, and if it makes them easier to eat, cut them into bite-size pieces and carry them in Ziploc bags. Always avoid foods that are sticky or create extra garbage (like peels and pits).

Whether you're traveling by car or plane, you'll also want to have plenty of drinks on hand. If you're going on a road trip, stock a cooler in the trunk with juice boxes and water bottles. When flying, once you've gone through security, buy enough drinks to at least tide you over until drinks are served on the plane.

You may want to consider bringing along a few extra treats to give in a pinch as a reward for good behavior. "I usually bring M&M'S," says Thorp. "If one of the kids is freaking out at 36,000 feet, I say, 'If you're really quiet and stay in your seat, I'll give you some M&M'S.' They're great in an emergency!"

TIP

**26**

# Choose your airline wisely.

Do your research and check what amenities and meals are provided or that can be purchased on your flight. It may affect which flight you decide to book as well as what items you decide to bring with you. For instance, if you don't have room in your bag for a portable DVD player (or you don't own one), you may want to consider booking with an airline that has in-flight entertainment systems on their planes.

"I love flying Virgin America," says Thorp. "I limit the amount of TV I let my kids watch at home, but if we're on vacation I let them watch as long as they want, and with the in-flight TVs, they'll sit there and won't move for hours!" Just remember to bring a set of headphones for each of your kids. Most airlines with in-flight entertainment systems provide them, but they may not fit your child's head properly.

Book direct flights whenever possible, and also check the airline's preboarding policies regarding children ahead of time. They differ per airline, and it's especially helpful to know when traveling with an infant.

If you're traveling with an infant, be aware that most airlines do allow you to bring your infant on the plane in a car seat, but be sure to double check with your airline to avoid any problems at the gate. The device must be an FAA-approved child safety seat and must be placed in a window seat on an aircraft with one aisle, and in either the window seat or the middle seat of a center section on planes with two aisles. So book your seats accordingly!

You can take your stroller with you to the gate, but it must be checked before you get on the plane. The stroller does not count as one of your carry-ons, and will be delivered to you plane-side when you arrive at your destination. Invest in a lightweight (yet sturdy!) collapsible stroller. Most stroller brands, including Britax and Bumbleride, make models that fold flat. If you're traveling with an infant and will be doing some driving on your trip, consider buying a stroller frame that your baby seat will snap into. Baby Trend, Graco, Jeep, and Maclaren all make them. You can also opt for a stroller that does double duty. "One of the best things I ever bought is this stroller called the Sit 'n' Stroll by Lilly Gold," says Thorp (www.lillygold.com). "It's a car seat that turns into a stroller and that fits in a seat on the plane. I can't rave enough about it!" You should also pack plenty of extra diapers and baby food or formula to carry on with you. These items are all tough to find in airport shops, so if your plane is delayed and you're stuck for several hours you'll be glad you have them!

TIP
27

# Plan to take tons of pictures & videos.

Be sure to bring whatever devices you use to take pictures and videos, along with their chargers, backup memory cards, and batteries.

If you want to share pictures with friends and family back home, think about investing in a camera with built-in Wi-Fi to make sharing on the go a cinch! Already have a camera you love, but isn't Wi-Fi enabled? Consider an Eye-Fi memory card (www.eye.fi). The company's enhanced SD cards allow you to wirelessly upload files from any camera or camcorder to your favorite sites (Facebook, Twitter, Picasa, YouTube), or to your phone, tablet, or computer.

TIP

# Save some toys for the trip home.

Not only is it important to have enough toys and games to last en route and while at your destination, but it's also imperative that you don't forget toys for the journey home! Bring along a few extra items and hide them away until the car ride or plane trip back home. Inexpensive items like stickers and coloring books are great bets!

## Packing List

- ☐ First-aid kit
- ☐ Handi Wipes
- ☐ Snacks (food and drinks)
- ☐ Toys and games
- ☐ Camera and/or camcorder

# Beach Vacations

WHAT YOU SHOULD CONSIDER BRINGING WITH YOU ON A BEACH VACA-
tion depends heavily on your mode of transportation. If you're flying to your destination, you will want to pack only the items you
cannot live without. Be smart about items that will be provided for
you or available for you rent or purchase.

When traveling by car, you have more options! You may choose
to bring your own towels, lounge chairs, your kids' favorite inflatable toys, or a large cooler for snacks and drinks. Once you've
packed the essentials, load up your trunk with fun extras. Just be
sure to restrict your items to the trunk and don't let too much stuff
overflow to the inside of your car. You want to be comfortable on
the ride over, not crammed in between all of your gear!

TIP

29

# Anticipate toting wet items.

Consider a wheelie bag designed
specifically for trips where water
is involved. Brands like Timbuk2
and Eagle Creek make versions
with separate lined pockets for
damp items like bathing suits.

When you're traveling by car
and have more room, an easy
way to carry wet items home is
in a heavy-duty garbage bag!
"Just dump all the wet towels,
bathing suits, and other items
in there—just remember to
dump them in the wash as soon

Bring some plastic bags with you
for packing wet or sandy swimsuits
and towels. Previous page: Haena
beach, on the Big Island of Hawaii.

as you get back home," says Elizabeth Thorp, founder of Posh-brood.com. Otherwise you will risk having mold grow on all your stuff!

Plastic grocery bags will also do the trick for smaller items like clothing and bathing suits, so it's always good to stash a few inside your beach tote. You might want to pick up a few reusable wet bags if you travel to the beach often. Planet Wise (http://planetwiseinc.com) makes zippered styles with more than one compartment.

TIP

**30**

# Go for brightly colored extras.

Don't forget to pack a roomy beach tote.

Opt for a beach tote in standout colors so it's easy to spot on a crowded beach when you're returning from taking a dip in the ocean. In addition to being eye-catching, the best beach totes are extra-roomy, with lots of pockets inside and out. Choose lightweight canvas, straw, mesh, or nylon. They're durable and easy to wipe clean, shake sand out of, or throw in the washing machine.

The same goes for towels and mats, too. If you're traveling by car and are bringing your own, choose ones in bright colors. Bring one for each member of your family and one extra. If you're flying, don't bring them—use the ones provided at your hotel or pick up a cheap one at your destination.

Another great item to bring if you're traveling by car is a soft, insulated tote for snacks and drinks. It's less bulky than a cooler and easier to carry with you to the beach. "I love Scout bags by Bungalow," says Thorp. "They make a whole bunch of cool, insulated totes that are super lightweight and the fabrics are so fun." You can find them at www.bungalowco.com.

TIP

31

# Keep your bathing suit with you.

You don't want to lose precious hours taking in the sun and sand if your luggage is lost or delayed—or if your hotel room isn't ready when you arrive. The most important item to have at the ready is your bathing suit, so never put it in your checked luggage! Either wear it on the plane or pack it in your carry-on and place it at the very top so you can just reach in and grab it without having fish around for it.

On top of your bathing suit wear items that you won't mind wearing to the beach. Men: Pair a T-shirt with shorts or khakis that you can roll up. Women: Capri pants and shorts also work with T-shirts and tank tops. Another foolproof outfit is a casual dress that can be worn as a coverup. If you tend to be cold on the plane, a maxidress is a smarter option over a short style. Wear a light sweater or pack it in your personal bag.

Pack at least one more bathing suit with you in addition to the one you wear or bring with you on the plane. That way you can alternate between the two while one is drying. Consider bringing a nicer one for walking around the resort and lounging by the pool and another suit that you don't mind wearing to actually swim, sit in the sand, or to wear to spa treatments if you decide to do so.

Pack at least two coverups to go along with each suit. A coverup can be whatever you don't mind going to the beach in, including lightweight (and light-colored, to avoid attracting heat) T-shirts, dresses, skirts, and sarongs. Pieces should be made of thin, cool fabrics like cotton or linen, and slip on and off easily.

In addition to your suits and coverups, bring breezy dresses, tops, and shorts. Choose prints and colors that complement each other so you can mix-and-match pieces. Even in the summer it's always good to have at least one pair of pants on hand. Avoid jeans in heavy denim. Instead go for cotton pants like khakis or cargoes, or lightweight denim in relaxed fits so that you don't overheat.

Have fun with accessories! Leave anything home that you'd be devastated to lose, but do bring jewelry like beaded bracelets, statement necklaces, fun hats, and sunglasses. They're an easy way to kick casual outfits up a notch, especially if you plan on going out to dinner or out dancing.

TIP
32

# Wear versatile shoes.

With the goal of being beach-ready on the plane in mind, wear sandals or slip-on canvas sneakers (TOMS, Converse, and Sanuk all make stylish options that are perfect for the beach). Go with sneakers if you want to keep your feet covered and stash a clean pair of socks in your personal bag for extra warmth.

If you do opt for sandals on the plane, be sure to bring a pair of stylish sneakers or sandals with you as well that can go straight from the beach to a restaurant (jeweled sandals are an easy way for women to add glamour to a beach outfit). Of course it's always a good idea to bring one pair of flip-flops, but you may want to stick to a pair in a neutral color like black, brown, or metallic gold or silver. They will be more versatile than a pair in a bright color and will work in many different settings.

TIP

33

# Cover your gadgets.

Be sure to protect any gadgets you decide to bring with you to the beach or pool from water and sand damage. It's the last thing you want to have to deal with on your trip! Keep items like your cellphone and camera either in a lined pocket of your beach tote or a separate waterproof camera case. Ziploc bags also work great, as do plastic makeup bags.

It's also a good idea to use waterproof covers whenever possible. M-Edge (www.medgestore.com) makes such cases for e-readers and tablets, and DiCAPac makes waterproof covers for cameras and cellphones. All allow you to actually use your gadget while it's in the case (except for the cellphone pouch—you can attempt to use it while it's inside, but you may find it quite difficult!). They're worth the peace of mind! A large Ziploc bag also works great for protecting your e-reader while you're using it.

You may also want to consider investing in gadgets that are actually waterproof. Companies like Kodak and Sony manufacture waterproof cameras and camcorders. You can also find waterproof speakers and MP3 players from brands like Speedo, H2O Audio, and Grace Digital Audio.

Airtight pouches, cases, and Ziploc bags are great for protecting your tech while you're outside, but be careful when returning to your air-conditioned hotel room. Moisture buildup in the bag caused by the change in temperature may damage your gadgets. As soon as you get inside, take items out of their bags and cases and allow them to cool until they reach room temperature before turning them on.

Leave your gadgets' accessories, including chargers, extra batteries, and memory cards in your car or hotel room to avoid damaging or losing them. Bring only what you need for that day along with you.

Also, if you have to take an item out of its protective cover in order to use it, do so sparingly. Even if you don't drop your gadget directly in the sand or the ocean, it may be damaged by sand kicked up by wind or splashing water. So it's best to keep them tucked away whenever possible.

TIP

## 34

# Cover yourself.

If you're headed to the beach, one of the most important things to think about is sun protection. At the very least, bring enough sunscreen to get you through the first few days of your trip. If you are going to be at your destination longer, it's usually best to just buy larger bottles while you're there. However, if you're checking luggage and have a bit of extra room (or if you're traveling by car) you may want to go ahead and bring your full-size bottles with you—resort areas often charge a premium for items like sunscreen.

When flying, you have a few TSA-friendly options. If you choose to bring **travel-size bottles,** you can go one of three ways: Buy individual bottles that are 3.4 ounces or less, pick up empty bottles and fill your own, or go for a prepackaged kit. Drugstores typically stock travel sizes of popular brands like Aveeno and Neutrogena. If you can't find the brand you like in a tiny bottle, buy an empty one and fill it yourself. At www.3floz.com you can find kits specifically made for the beach that include liquid sunscreen, lip balm with SPF, towelettes, and more—everything you need for a weekend at the beach!

**Sunscreen towelettes** (wipes that are premoistened with sunscreen) are another great option. They're easy to use and they won't count toward your allotted liquids. So they're an especially smart option when you're flying. Check out the brand Supergoop! (www.supergoop.com) for these. They make packages in different sizes, including individually wrapped, single-use packets.

When you're packing bottles of liquid sunscreen (especially if you're toting full-size bottles), be sure to pack them carefully. Not only do you want to prevent them from exploding all over your clothes, but you want to prevent them from exploding at all! Even if the mess is contained inside a Ziploc bag, it's still a mess. Avoid this by placing a couple of pieces of tape over the top of each of your bottles. Remove the tape as soon as you arrive so that it's easy to peel off. The longer it sits, especially if it's out in the sun for a bit, the harder it will be to get off. Once you've taped each of your bottles, place them in a Ziploc bag. Don't pack them in a fancy toiletry bag! Disposable airtight bags work just as well and you can just discard them if there are any mishaps.

Bring sunscreen that is suitable for your body and face. If you have sensitive skin you'll want to bring separate formulas for both. Also, if your skin is sensitive you should probably stick to your tried-and-true sunscreen instead of switching it up and using a new one for the first time at your destination. Irritated skin is an easy way to put a damper on your trip! If you're going on a longer trip and have a sunscreen you can't live without, you may want to check your bag or fill several small bottles with the same sunscreen to get you through the duration of your trip.

Don't forget to also think about lip balm with SPF, too. Lips burn easily! Bring your own or plan to purchase a stick once you've arrived.

# Choose proper eye & head gear.

Okay, so you've got sunscreen for your face, lips, and body taken care of; now it's time to take a look at protection for your eyes! Bring at least one pair of sunglasses with you, but if you have room, it's always good to have a backup pair. Pick shades that have 99% UVA and UVB ray protection, especially when you're wearing them outside for prolonged periods of time. Unless it's a brand you trust, ignore those "UV protection" stickers. They aren't regulated, so anyone can slap one on! Instead, get them tested by an optician (it's usually free) to make sure they're safe. Also, treat them like sunscreen and wear them at all times on the beach, even if it's overcast.

Hats are also great to wear on the beach for added sun protection. Go for a chic straw hat or a lightweight cotton or canvas version. Brands like San Diego Hat Company (www.sandiegohat.com) make stylish, versatile options that are specially made to block UV rays.

## Packing List

- ☐ Bathing suits (2)
- ☐ Sunscreen
- ☐ Bag for wet bathing suit
- ☐ Waterproof bags or cases for electronics
- ☐ Flip-flops
- ☐ Sunglasses

# Road Trips

CAR EXCURSIONS ARE A GREAT WAY TO EXPLORE AND TAKE A BREAK from the hassles of air travel. You don't have to worry about security checkpoints, bag size and weight limits, restricted items, hidden fees—essentially, you can just get in your car and go, right? Almost, but not quite! It's still a good idea to thoughtfully plan what you're going to bring and how you're going to pack it in your car. After all, you will be spending a good bit of time in your vehicle, which can feel cramped, especially if you're traveling with a group! So as with other trip types, the more you prepare ahead of time, the more smoothly your trip will go. Bring things that will make your trip as comfortable as possible, keep you on the correct route to your destination, and that will prevent an emergency like a flat tire from turning into a trip-derailing disaster!

TIP

36

# Leave boxy suitcases at home.

When it comes to packing your clothes for a road trip, you basically want to do the opposite of what you do when flying. Since you're not dealing with the airlines' rules and restrictions, there's no need to cram all of your stuff into one back-straining 50-pound bag! So avoid structured suitcases—they aren't necessary and will take up a lot of space in your trunk. Instead, spread your stuff out over several smaller, soft-sided bags like duffel bags and backpacks. They can be stuffed under seats and into corners and other small spaces, which will make it easier to actually pack the trunk, and they will be easier to shift as you go. It will also come in handy when making pit stops along the way. Plus, they can be stashed in the back seat when needed.

Think about your route and where you will stop along the way. If you plan on stopping for at least one night, pack an overnight bag. Fill a small backpack or duffel with only the items you will need to use that night, including a change of clothes, pajamas, toiletries,

Previous page: A classic Chevy cruising to Las Vegas.

Soft duffel bags like this one are easy to squish into the corners of your trunk.

medications, and any other personal items. That way you won't have to dig through all of your stuff to make sure you have everything and you will avoid having to lug all of your bags to the room for just one night. Do the same for each family member. If you're all staying in one room, consider consolidating your bags. For example, pack you and your partner's items in one bag and your kids' things in another. Place your overnight bags near the top of the trunk for easy access.

Pack the rest of your items—the things that you will only plan on using after you've arrived at your final destination—in a duffel bag or weekender bag that's larger than your overnight bag. Spread your family's things out over a few different bags. These should go in the back of the trunk to save room for up front for the items that you will use en route.

When putting items in your trunk, don't just throw everything in there haphazardly. Packing your trunk should be like fitting pieces of a puzzle together—you want to place things carefully and strategically so you can find things easily. Start by gathering everything you're taking with you and survey what you've got. Sort items into two categories: things you will need to use en route and items you won't need to use until you reach your final destination. Unless something is fragile, place items you won't use along the way in the bottom and the back of the trunk. The bulkiest, heaviest items (such as ski or camping gear) should go on the very bottom. Put things that you will use along the way (day bags, cooler) on top so you don't have to dig for them. Know exactly where your roadside emergency kit and gear are and make sure you can get to them easily in a pinch. Fill in gaps between items with small items and soft-sided luggage.

TIP

**37**

# Go for supercomfy outfits.

Since you will be sitting for a long period of time, comfort should be your number one priority! Wear soft, roomy pieces in breathable fabric. Cotton blends and jersey are great options. Avoid items like jeans (the heavy denim may be uncomfortable and will take forever to dry if something is spilled on it) and light-colored clothing that will show dirt and stains easily.

Think about where you'll be stopping along the way. Especially if you're planning to stop at a nicer restaurant or hotel, keep that in mind when deciding what to wear. You can't go wrong with simple, unfussy outfits. Breezy dresses and leggings paired with tunics are great options for women. Cotton twill chinos or trousers and T-shirts are good choices for men. If you do prefer to wear jeans, choose a lightweight pair in a dark wash to hide stains.

Be prepared for weather changes by dressing in layers, but skip bulky items that will cause you to overheat in the car. Have a sweater and rain gear (such a light windbreaker) handy, either in the back seat or in the trunk, in case of inclement weather.

TIP

**38**

# Wear shoes that fit well.

Just like your clothes, comfort is key when it comes to choosing the shoes for your next road trip—especially if you're the driver! "Avoid shoes that may easily slip off your feet, such as flip-flops or sandals without straps to keep them secure," says AAA spokesperson Heather Hunter. "Wear shoes that are comfortable on your feet—not too tight or ill fitting." It's also important to take into consideration that "some people's feet may swell slightly when seated for a long period of time, so make sure the shoes won't restrict or cut into the feet too much in case they do swell during the trip," says Hunter. Sneakers, loafers, driving shoes, and sandals that securely strap to your feet (but that aren't too tight) are all great options.

If you're a passenger, it's also important to keep the same things in mind, but you do have a bit more flexibility because you don't have to worry about driving. Choose comfy shoes that slip on and off easily. You might want to consider going with shoes that don't have laces. They will be easier to take them off if you want to wiggle your toes for a few minutes or change to a different pair of shoes along the way.

TIP
39

# Don't rely (totally) on your gadgets.

GPS units are invaluable on road trips, especially if you're driving through unfamiliar territory. They will can help navigate around traffic, find nearby rest stops, recalculate your route if you accidentally get off course, and much more. So definitely bring along a GPS if you have one. If you're renting a car and don't own one, you may want to consider a rental. "Many car-rental companies offer GPS units for rent as well," says Hunter.

That said, it's extremely important that you do not rely completely on your GPS! Like any gadget, it may malfunction or it may provide you with incorrect information. So be prepared and research your route and your destination ahead of time. Bring along printed maps and directions to guide you in case your GPS can't. Map out exactly where you want to go and how you want to get there, and pinpoint sights you want to see along the way and places you might want to stop for the night. While you don't have to book hotels ahead of time, especially if you want to have the flexibility to be spontaneous or to stop when the driver is tired, you should familiarize yourself with towns and hotels along your route. Know general availability so you're not stuck jumping from one fully booked hotel to another.

Make sure you have a list of emergency numbers with you as well. While it's a great idea to program them into your cellphone, you should keep a hard copy of the numbers in your glove compartment as well.

If you have a smartphone, take advantage of its capabilities and load up useful apps before you go, too. There are tons of apps

Technology is great, but make sure you research your route and bring some maps, too.

that can help make your trip go more smoothly, from rest-stop finders to fun games for your kids. Just be sure to complete any downloads, including movies for your iPad or laptop, before you leave home while you have a reliable Internet connection.

Along with wall chargers, it's also helpful to bring along extra batteries and car chargers so that you can keep your tech powered up at all times. Consider investing in a universal car charger with different connectors (including USB and micro USB ports) so that you can charge all of your gadgets with one device. Brands like Philips and TomTom make versatile models. Before you leave, test out your car chargers on each of your gadgets to make sure they work properly together.

Another connector you might want to look into is one for your iPod, iPhone, or MP3 player that will allow you to play the music on the devices through your car's stereo system. Depending on your car's capabilities, you may just need a simple cord. If your car is not equipped with a special port for this, there are plenty of other options to look into such as auxiliary cables and FM transmitters. Look into this before you leave in case you need to call the dealer or visit a store like Best Buy to learn about the different options that are available to you.

You can stash small gadgets and chargers in the glove compartment, but if you're carrying several you might want to consider packing them in a soft-side tote or special travel case for added protection. GPS carrying cases often have extra room and multiple compartments, so you may be able to stash additional gadgets and cords in there. Also check out organizers from CaseLogic—they offer cases in all different shapes and sizes, with options specifically designed for car travel. Whatever you pack your gear in, keep it with you in the car for easy access.

# Tote a fully stocked cooler.

Carve out space for a hard-sided cooler in your trunk. Choose the size of the cooler according to how much space you have in your trunk and the number of people traveling in your car. Be especially generous with the snacks if you're traveling with kids; a well-timed box of raisins may very well circumvent a total meltdown!

Fill the cooler with items that are easy to eat on the go. Stay away from foods that require any kind of preparation and that are messy to eat, including sticky foods, those that crumble easily, or items with powdery toppings like confectioner's sugar. Instead, bring foods that are compact, easy to eat, and can be packed in individual servings. Fruit and vegetables are perfect for road trips! Grapes and baby carrots are good bets. Other fruits and veggies, including apples, oranges, celery, and cucumbers are also a yummy, healthy snack to have on hand, but peel and cut them into small bite-size pieces before you go. Pack all items in individual Ziploc bags.

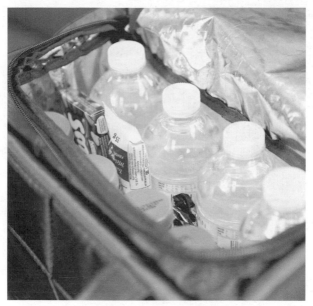

Keep a small cooler, like this one, up front for snacking as you go.

If you want to bring along certain perishable items, such as pre-made turkey sandwiches (hold the mustard and the mayo—instead, bring packets and add them later so the bread won't get soggy) and cheese, just be sure there is enough ice in your cooler to keep them thoroughly cooled. Don't wait too long because you don't want these items to go bad and cause you to get sick along the way! Consider planning a spot to have a picnic within the first couple of hours of your trip.

Also bring along nonperishable or individually wrapped foods like granola bars, fruit snacks, potato chips, popcorn (can be popped ahead of time and placed in small Ziploc bags), and pre-packaged cookies and crackers.

Don't forget the drinks! Stick to liquids that are clear—they will be much easier to clean up if someone spills. You can't go wrong with bottled water. Consider getting reusable water bottles with built-in filters (such as the ones from Bobble; www.waterbobble. com) to refill along the way. If you want to bring juice, you might want to go with juice boxes. Even if the juice is a lighter color, the juice boxes will help prevent spills and are great for kids. Always avoid drinks that are impossible to remove from clothing and upholstery, like grape and cherry juice. Keep in mind that soda can create a sticky mess if spilled! If your crew can't make it through the trip without something sweet and fizzy, opt for a light-colored brand like Sprite.

Once you've stocked your cooler for the trunk, fill a small soft-sided cooler to keep with you in the car. Pack it with a couple of drinks and a few snacks so that you don't have to keep pulling over every five minutes to access the one in the trunk, especially on long stretches in between towns, gas stations, and rest areas. Each time you do stop, restock it with supplies. Replace foods and drinks that were consumed or rotate out items that are no longer cool.

TIP
41

# Make cleanup a cinch.

This is particularly important when you're traveling with kids, but adults create messes, too! Carry an arsenal of supplies with you, including premoistened wipes (consider moist towelettes for your hands and Lysol wipes for cleaning the car), paper towels, and bags for trash. Plastic grocery bags are great for this—the handles are convenient and they can easily be stuffed places so that they are always within reach. Always stash extras in the trunk, but have some of each of these items with you in the car at all times.

In the trunk, you might want to set up a collapsible laundry hamper or a fabric-covered organization crate, especially if you're traveling with toys, sports equipment, or destination-specific gear (such as inflatable toys and towels for the beach). You can use egg crates for this, too. They're great for managing small items and you can throw soiled clothing in them as well. Then all you have to do when you get back home is take the hamper or crate straight to the laundry room!

TIP
42

# Check your emergency kit.

Don't just assume that everything is in working order! Just like you should get your car checked out before each road trip, you should also check each of the items in your emergency kit. Make sure the batteries in your flashlight are working (if you're not positive exactly how fresh they are, go ahead and replace them and bring extras), that the spare tire hasn't deflated, and that items in your first-aid kit haven't expired. Thoroughly check each and every item so that you're 100% sure everything is ready to go.

Take care in packing your emergency kit. Most items will last quite a long time, so you'll really only have to do the bulk of the work once. According to Hunter, most emergency kits for road trips should include

- Jumper cables
- Blanket
- Bottled water
- Nonperishable food
- Basic hand tools (screwdriver, adjustable wrench)
- Cloth or paper towels
- Flares, an emergency beacon, or reflective triangles
- Emergency road service information, including any membership info (such as AAA)
- Tire pressure gauge
- First-aid kit
- Flashlight
- Extra batteries

"During the winter it's a good idea to update the kit with additional items," says Hunter. "Include sand, cat litter or traction mats, an ice scraper, snow brush, hand warmers, gloves, a hat, and additional warm clothes."

## Packing List

☐ GPS unit
☐ Road map
☐ Cleaning supplies
☐ Cooler with snacks
☐ Emergency kit

# Cruises

The average standard cabin on a cruise ship is less than 200 square feet, so pay careful attention to the square footage when booking and packing for your cruise. It's important to bring certain items, and pack in such a way that will help you adapt to the smaller space. Otherwise, cruises are meant to be relaxing, fun, and all-inclusive! So you only need to make sure you bring your basic gear.

TIP
43

# Don't worry about lugging your bag.

"A cruise is different because you're not schlepping your suitcase, lugging it up and down steps on a train, so feel free to bring whichever suitcase you want," says Carolyn Spencer Brown, Editor in Chief of Cruisecritic.com. "Of course that depends on if you're traveling by car or plane and whether or not you want to check your bag, but cruises are increasingly designing cabins with room underneath beds to accommodate larger bags."

If you do choose to bring a larger suitcase, take into account your actual cabin size and check with your cruise line to see if there will be space to store it. If there isn't space, pack your things in smaller, soft-side bags, like rolling duffels, backpacks and totes, that can be flattened and stuffed into corners after you unpack them. You can always bring several of these if needed.

Keep in mind that there are closets in most cabins, but it is unlikely that they will be stocked with enough hangers to accommodate all of your clothing. So if you plan to completely unpack your bags (which is something you will definitely want to do if you are going on a cruise longer than 2 or 3 days) you may want to consider bringing several extra hangers with you. They're lightweight and can be packed at the very bottom of your suitcase.

Previous page: *The Sapphire Princess* in Sitka, Alaska.

Make sure your day bag can hold everything you'll need for your first several hours on board the ship. A soft-sided, collapsible wheelie bag is a good choice for a cruise, because cabin storage space is limited.

In addition to your suitcase, bring a day bag for ports of call and to carry essentials to different activities around the ship. When boarding, treat your day bag as your carry-on bag. "The first day you check your luggage at the check-in desk, and you're most likely going to be without your bags for about 6 to 8 hours," says Brown. "So pack anything you're going to need for the day, like your bathing suit, sunscreen, and any medications you need to take."

TIP

44

# Board wearing a resort-casual outfit.

It's also important to keep the fact that you'll be without your luggage for a while in mind when picking your outfit to wear the first day. "Make sure whatever you're wearing is comfortable. I suggest aiming for resort casual because whatever you're wearing when you board may even need to take you into the evening, especially if there are delays delivering your baggage to your cabin," says Brown. "But the first night of dinner is always casual. People are still getting their luggage and most will not have unpacked."

Resort casual is basically a step up from super-casual clothes like cutoff shorts, tanks, T-shirts, and flip-flops. When in doubt, just stick to classic styles in neutral colors or bright colors and patterns that transition easily from day to night. Consider wearing an easy dress or a pair of khaki or black pants with a blouse or a polo shirt. Save your extra casual clothes for later, but if you think you'll want them on the first day (for instance, if you plan to hit the pool immediately after you board), just pack them in your tote or personal bag.

TIP

45

# Check the dress code.

"It used to be that you had to pack for all different occasions—formal, semiformal, evening—but the dress code has been simplified. It's a lot more relaxed in the evening than it used to be. Now most cruise lines stick to a casual dress code most of the time," says Brown. "Even if they do have formal nights, if you don't want to participate, you can just eat at a different restaurant that night. You won't see many people wearing jeans or shorts in the dining room at night, but during the day, anything goes." In general, a jersey dress, easy skirt, or casual slacks will work for dinner, along with a pair of strappy sandals or loafers.

There are, however, several cruise lines that take formal nights seriously. "Cunard and Crystal Cruises are both lines where people dress more formally. Princess and Carnival are two others where people get excited about getting all dolled up on formal nights," says Brown. "Even on some Disney cruises, there are dress-up nights where parents will dress their little boys in tuxedos, and little girls in princess dresses—it's a really fun and special ambiance." Know that dress codes do vary on each ship in a company's fleet. Most cruise lines have detailed descriptions of dress codes on their websites and a quick Internet search pulls up lots of useful information, including forums, on this topic. It's important to do your research ahead of time, because you may want to pick your cruise based on which dress code you prefer. But on the other hand, nearly all cruises offer some sort of casual dining service and room service, so you can certainly avoid formal dinners if you want to.

It's always best to leave valuables at home, but if you do want to bring jewelry (perhaps to wear on formal nights), most ships have safes in each cabin, so you can stash them there along with your passport and extra cash.

TIP

46

# Make a list of activities beforehand.

In addition to the clothes for dinner and formal nights if needed, bring clothes according types of activities you plan to participate in, on the ship and at ports of call. Do you want to spend lots of time at the pool? If so, bring a couple of bathing suits and coverups, flip-flops and plenty of sunscreen. Do you want to exercise? Be sure to bring comfortable athletic shoes and workout clothes. Do you plan on participating in shore excursions? When booking them, make a list of any additional gear you will need to supply yourself so that you don't end up having to miss out.

"As far as clothing, I typically bring three of everything and use the ship's laundry service if needed," says Brown. "It's usually reasonably priced, and some ships even have self-service laundry you can use in a pinch." Always dress in layers in case you're too hot or cold. Bring a light sweater or jacket in case the air-conditioning is too much for comfort.

Don't forget to bring your own reading material with you as well. "Most cruise ships only have a very small library, if there's one at all," says Brown. And you'll want to have something on hand for leisurely afternoons at sea.

TIP

47

# Be prepared for small bathrooms.

Small cabins mean cramped bathrooms, so pack your toiletries in a hanging toiletry bag. If you're sharing the bathroom with other people, you might want to even bring along a fabric hanging shoe caddy that folds up flat when not in use. "Put it over the back of your door and let each person keep their stuff in their own compartment," says Brown. "It's a smart way to stay organized!"

Most cruise lines offer basic toiletries, including lotion, shampoo, and conditioner, but that's about it, so it's always good to

Hanging toiletry bags come in very handy in tiny cruise ship bathrooms.

Consider packing a travel alarm clock— most ships don't offer them.

bring your own, especially if you're particular about which products and brands you use. "Every ship has some sort of small shop for toiletries, so if you forget stuff you can always buy things there. They typically even have items like underwear and socks," says Brown. If you use a blow-dryer regularly, consider bringing your own—"the blow-dryers provided on ships are always weak!"

Also, because of their size, most cabins are equipped with just one outlet. "So if you have several devices you're going to want to use and charge at once, like your phone, Kindle, blow-dryer, music player, electric shaver, and iPad, bring your own power strip," says Brown. "Cruise lines don't advocate this, but it's a good item to bring along so you're covered in case you need it." An outlet multiplier will also do the trick.

## Packing List

- ☐ Day bag
- ☐ Dressy dinner outfit (if needed)
- ☐ Bathing suit
- ☐ Hanging toiletry bag (or shoe caddy)
- ☐ Kindle
- ☐ Power strip

# Outdoor Adventure Trips: Warm Weather

NO MATTER IF YOU'RE A FIRST-TIMER OR A SEASONED PRO, FITTING ALL of the necessary gear for a safari or a hiking, biking, canoeing, camping, or kayaking trip into your suitcase can be difficult. It's all about maximizing space and making sure you have the proper clothing and equipment.

"The saying we have in the industry is that there's no bad weather, just bad gear!" says Dan Austin, director of Austin-Lehman Adventures. So do your research and invest in quality items, especially when it comes to protecting yourself from the elements and possible injury.

TIP

48

# Get properly fitted for a backpack.

No matter the size or type of backpack, it's extremely important to find the best one to suit your needs and your body. An ill-fitting backpack can cause back pain, muscle strain, or nerve damage. "Do your homework and decide what you're going to use your backpack for," says Austin. "Take your time and go to a good outfitter where they have a staff that knows the nuances of the different packs." Head to a store like REI, Dick's Sporting Goods, or Eastern Mountain Sports and have them take your hip and torso measurements. They can also help you sort through all of the different styles and features—from zip-off day packs and hydration packs to top-loading zippers and interchangeable straps—to find the backpack that best suits your needs. Your research will definitely pay off each time you use your backpack, especially when it comes to comfort and convenience.

When packing your backpack, a general rule to follow is to "put the things you don't need en route on the bottom, along with items that will compress, like a big puffy down jacket. You can always

Previous page: Hiking the Coromandel Coastal Walkway in New Zealand.

redistribute things when you get there," says Austin. "On top, pack a light windbreaker jacket, a hat, and gloves in case you need them right when you arrive."

Place over-size or oddly shaped items on the outside of the pack to free up space on the inside. For example, clip a bike helmet to an outside hook or strap and stuff bulky shoes into outside pockets.

"If your backpack is small enough to take with you on the plane, pack it like you would a typical carry-on, with items like your wallet, medications, Kindle, and so on," says Austin.

Take your time picking out the backpack that will work best for your trip.

TIP
49

# Opt for quick-dry fabrics.

"Pick lightweight fabrics that will wick moisture away from your body, will dry quickly if washed by hand, and can be layered when needed," says Austin. Whether you shop sportswear brands or fashion brands, look for synthetic fabrics like polyester-spandex blends and microfiber, and always avoid heavy fabrics like 100% cotton and denim. Brands like ExOfficio, Columbia Sportswear, and Nike all make clothes that are specifically made to repel moisture, but you can also find clothes that will work at stores such as Target or Old Navy. Dig around in your closet a bit, too! You may find you already own items (even if they aren't sport specific) that are suitable to wear as well. Check tags for fabric content and try on each item. Move around in them a bit to make sure they fit comfortably and do not restrict your movement in any way.

Depending on what activities you will be participating in on your trip, you also may want to consider water-resistant or waterproof clothing and shoes (Gore-Tex makes these items for every activity) or items that are UPF-rated.

UPF-rated clothing is specially made to block out the sun's harmful rays. It works like sunscreen that you don't need to reapply. You can find UPF-rated clothing at sporting goods stores. Columbia makes a wide range of UPF-rated clothing and accessories.

TIP

50

# Be prepared for cool weather.

Even though you're heading to a warm climate, you should always plan for cooler temperatures just in case. Bring lots of clothes that you can layer—a thin jacket, long-sleeve shirt, or scarf should do the trick. You may want to consider pants that are convertible, with legs that can be unzipped at the knees and turned into shorts depending on the temperature.

# Wear your bulkiest shoes on the plane.

Most likely these will be your hiking or biking shoes. Even if they have laces, the extra space in your bag is worth the extra few minutes it will take you to get them off and on at security. In addition to biking and hiking shoes, "I always like to bring a pair of Tevas because you can wear them as water shoes, and as casual shoes when you're not on the trail," says Austin.

Only bring shoes that fit well and are very comfortable. If you're buying new shoes specifically for your trip, keep in mind that while some shoes may require a short break-in time, they should

Lined wet bags can come in very handy on backpacking trips.

still be comfortable from the moment you put them on in the store. Walk around in them a bit and see how they feel. "If they're not comfortable on 20 feet of carpet, they won't be comfortable on miles of trails," says Austin. "Newer boots and shoes made of synthetic fabric shouldn't need a lot of break-in time, but if at all possible, put them to the test before you leave on similar terrain as what you will encounter on your trip."

In addition, it's always good to invest in a good pair of socks to help cut down on blisters. You also may want to wear sock liners as well. They're made to be worn underneath your socks and are made of ultrathin, lightweight, moisture-wicking fabrics. They will help keep your feet dry and cut down on the friction between your skin and outer socks, which will help prevent blisters.

# Leave your flip-flops at home.

"Flip-flops are limited," says Austin. "If you go on a rafting trip, they'll fall right off!" Although they don't take up too much space, every inch is considered precious real estate when packing a backpack (or any bag for that matter). So opt for a good pair of secure water shoes instead. Strappy pairs from Teva or Jambu are good bets.

# Make a list.

Do your research ahead of time and list out all of the items specific to your trip that you will need. Some items you might want to consider bringing include bed liners, sleeping bags, sport gloves, a cover for your pack, ear plugs, and wet bags. Just remember: Your goal is to travel as light as possible, so stick to the items that are absolutely essential! With each and every item ask yourself if you *really* need it, and how often you will use it.

One item that is always good to bring is a good head lamp with a bright light. "It doubles as a flashlight and a reading light, so it will always come in handy no matter where you're going!" says Austin. "Plus, they're small and compact."

TIP
54

# Hand wash items along the way.

Don't forget to bring some laundry supplies.

Also ask yourself "How many times will I wear this?" about each item. If the answer is "once," then don't bring it. You should plan to wear every item that goes into your bag at least two times.

Washing as you go will allow you to wear each item of clothing several times throughout your trip, even if they get soiled or stained. To do this, pack a bit of clothes-line or twine sturdy enough to hold your clothes while they dry. It's perfectly okay to use the same soap you plan to bathe in on your clothes, but if you're worried about running out of it, or would simply like to bring along additional soap, consider travel-size packets from a brand like Soak (www.soakwash.com) or Eucalan (www.eucalan.com). Both are no-rinse washes, which means they're super easy to use, and will come in handy when water is in limited supply.

If you've already packed your maximum limit for carry-on liquids, packets of powdered soap are great options. Dryer sheets are good to have on hand as well. They're fantastic for freshening up clothes in a pinch, and they'll make your entire suitcase or backpack smell great. Plus, they don't take up space in your bag or add to your liquids. Place a few in a small zip-top bag, squeeze the air out, and slip it in between two items of clothing. Whenever you want to refresh or deodorize a garment, just rub the fabric with the sheet and it'll smell like freshly washed laundry. You'll be able to use one sheet several times before tossing it.

Being able to clean and freshen items quickly and efficiently throughout your trip will allow you to bring more items that will serve a dual purpose (and wear them freely without having to worry about it), such as a sarong that can be used as a beach coverup and a scarf or wrap.

TIP
55

# Downsize your toiletries.

Don't weigh yourself down with big bottles. You can either buy prepackaged travel sizes or buy empty bottles and fill your own. If you're going on an extended trip, pack enough to get you through the first few days and buy larger bottles when you get there.

In addition to your toothpaste and toothbrush, always bring (or buy at your destination) hand sanitizer and sunscreen. "Hand sanitizer is invaluable no matter where you are traveling," says Austin. Choose a sunscreen that best suits your needs, whether it's waterproof or has a high SPF.

TIP

## 56

# Protect yourself.

"A painful blister can ruin your trip, so you definitely want to bring a good blister kit," says Austin. "You used to have to put them together yourself, but now you can buy them with everything already in it." A typical blister kit includes hand soap, antiseptic ointment, gauze, and moleskin.

Also be sure to bring a well-stocked first-aid kit with plenty of bandages in all different shapes and sizes. "It also never hurts to have some Imodium or Tums, along with an immune system booster like Airborne or vitamin C. Whenever you're traveling, and especially while on an adventure trip where you're going to be active, you definitely don't want to get sick!" Austin.

Guard against potentially harmful bug bites with a good insect repellant. Like your toiletries, bring just enough to get you through the first few days of your trip and plan to buy more along the way. Especially if you're going to be in places with lots of bugs like mosquitoes, you're going to want to reapply often, so you will definitely need more bug spray than you can bring in a carry-on. You may want to consider a heavy-duty product that contains DEET, a highly effective active ingredient that is found in many kinds of bug repellent. According to the CDC (Centers for Disease Control and Prevention), the percentage of DEET you should look for depends on the amount of time you plan to be outdoors. Visit the CDC's website for more information on DEET, as well as vaccinations and other health precautions that must be taken when traveling to certain areas of the world.

# Bring your own helmet for a biking trip.

"On a bike trip I like to bring my own helmet," says Austin. "That way I know it's comfortable and it fits. Plus, it can be clipped to the outside of your pack so it won't take up space inside your bag."

It's also a good idea to bring your own biking gloves. They'll protect your skin, improve your grip and control over the bike, and they'll help absorb shock, especially if you take a tumble.

# Stick to neutral-colored clothing for a safari.

When planning outfits for a safari, think neutral colors like beige, khaki, and army green. These colors reflect the sun's rays and will also blend into the environment. Avoid dark colors like brown, black, and navy that will absorb heat and stand out. Also opt for lightweight, breathable fabrics. Pack plenty of layers, and don't forget a hat and binoculars!

## Packing List

☐ Good hiking shoes
☐ First-aid and blister kits
☐ Rain jacket and pants
☐ Head lamp
☐ Sunscreen
☐ Bug repellant with DEET

# Outdoor Adventure Trips: Cold Weather

THE MOST CHALLENGING THING ABOUT GOING ON A SKI OR SNOW-boarding trip is figuring out what to take with you, what to leave home, and what to rent at your destination.

When traveling by plane, keep in mind that most airlines will allow you to check one ski bag or snowboard, plus one boot bag per person, but extra baggage fees, weight limits, and size restrictions vary per airline. So if you plan to check equipment, call or check the airline's website *before* you book your ticket so that there are no surprises!

# Bring a sturdy suitcase.

Consider a hard-sided suitcase that will resist water better than ballistic nylon. Also look at wheelie duffel bags.

"The one thing I wouldn't scrimp on is a good carry-on suitcase with wheels, that maximizes the carry-on requirements," says Austin. "Pick one that is expandable and has sturdy wheels and zippers." Look at companies like REI, Eagle Creek, Timbuk2, and Burton. They all make ultrasturdy bags in different sizes and styles (including great wheelie duffel bags) specifically made to hold up well on rugged adventure trips.

Previous page: Admiring the view from the Zugspitze, Germany's tallest mountain.

# Rent ski & snowboarding equipment at your destination.

Not only will this cut down on the hassle of lugging heavy, bulky gear, but it might also prove to be cost effective. Most airlines allow you to check one ski or snowboard bag plus one boot bag in place of one checked bag, but of course you have to pay the extra baggage fees and are restricted to weight and size limits (these vary per airline) or else you'll be hit with even more fees! Keep in mind that you will have to pay the additional fees at least twice—once on your way there and again on your flight back home. And in addition to the hefty extra fees, there is the potential cost of replacing or repairing items that are lost or damaged en route. So do your research: In many cases you will be able to rent the latest equipment on-site, and not pay much more than you'd pay in airline fees if you brought your own gear.

# Stash small accessories in your boot bag.

If you do decide to bring your own boots instead of renting them at your destination, they're easiest to lug packed in a boot bag. If you are traveling by plane, take full advantage of any extra space inside the bag and stow accessories like goggles, hand warmers, extra socks, and gloves (and if you carry it on board with you, keep in mind that it will count as your personal item).

The bucket boot bag from High Sierra has extra room for accessories.

In addition to your ski or snowboard boots, "it's also always good to bring a good trail runner that can double as a tennis shoe," says Austin. "A lot of them are waterproof and don't require a lot of break-in time, so even if you buy them right before your trip, you don't have to worry about trashing your feet with a new pair of shoes."

Invest in a few pairs of warm, high-quality wool socks. Liners are great to have as well. "SmartWool's liner is amazing, and you can wear it with any sock," says Austin. It will keep your feet warm and help prevent blisters (www.smartwool.com).

TIP
62

# Never check items that you can't afford to do without.

"Nothing will ruin a weekend ski trip faster than losing your first 2 days of gear in a delayed checked bag!" says Austin. "Always think about your must-have items—what you'll need to get through the first couple of days, such as your warmest clothing, gloves, goggles, and helmet—and pack those items in your carry-on."

Layering is key, so start with a good base layer and go from there. Look for snug-fitting tops and long underwear in synthetic, moisture-wicking materials like polyester blends, or natural fabrics like merino wool or silk. Avoid base layers that are 100% cotton because they will absorb sweat and keep it close to your skin.

On top of your base layers you'll want to add clothing that will provide insulation, such as a sweater made of fleece or Polartec or a slim goose down vest. Lastly, you'll want an outer layer that protects you from the cold, wind, rain, and snow. This can be a jacket or a shell that is waterproof or water-resistant (depending on your needs). Be sure to also bring a good pair of gloves and a hat.

Also, it's easy to get caught up in focusing on making sure you have enough gear for when you're on the slopes, so don't forget to pack clothing to wear around the resort, such as pajamas and loungewear.

TIP
63

# Carry your coat with you on the plane.

Your coat is your warmest layer, so even if it's too hot for you to wear en route, bring it with you on the plane—you don't want to risk being without it if your luggage gets lost. "It can double as a nice pillow!" says Austin.

It's also a great idea to bring along a thin rain jacket. Pack that in your carry-on as well. "So many times I've ended up putting all of my layers on with my rain jacket on top, because not only will it protect you from water, but it will also break down wind and cut the cold," says Austin.

TIP
64

# Store your electronics in protective cases.

Make sure your gadgets are protected from being damaged as much as possible. Consider investing in shock-absorbing cases that are specially designed to take a beating. Companies like Ballistic (www.goballisticcase.com) make cellphone and tablet cases made of impact-resistant polycarbonate.

You also might want to invest in "sports" or "tough" versions of your most-used items like your camera or camcorder. Most electronics brands make them, including Kodak, Olympus, and Sony. You'll find models that are waterproof, shockproof, and even ones that are built to withstand extreme temperatures.

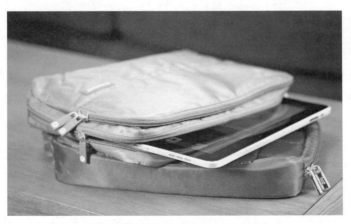

Make sure you give your electronics some extra protection.

## Packing List

☐ Heavy coat
☐ Rain jacket
☐ Wool socks
☐ Hand warmers
☐ Hat and gloves

# City Trips

TRAVEL TO ANY MAJOR METROPOLITAN CITY AROUND THE WORLD, from New York to London to Milan, presents similar packing challenges. You may be asking yourself these questions: How do I stay comfortable but look at least somewhat stylish? How can I guard my stuff against pickpockets? What's the best way to get around the city with my stuff in tow? You're not alone! Most travelers ask themselves similar questions, and they're all good to keep in mind when prepping for your city trip.

TIP

65

# Look for easy-to-maneuver luggage.

"Definitely bring a wheelie bag! You don't want to have to lug a duffel doing things like getting in and out of taxis," says Melanie Fascitelli, Founder of Clos-ette and Clos-ette Too. Suitcases with four wheels instead of two—they're called spinners—are great for navigating crowded streets and they're super easy to maneuver on escalators. Most luggage companies make them, including Samsonite, Tumi, American Tourister, and Bric's. Always go for a bag that's expandable. An inch or two of extra room may prove to be a lifesaver!

If you're checking luggage, pack enough clothing in your carry-on to last you a couple of days in case your bags are lost or delayed. Also bring a day bag, such as a crossbody or messenger bag, to carry with you while you're out exploring. If it's not big enough to hold everything you want to have with you on the plane, carry it inside a larger tote and take it out once you've reached your destination.

Previous page: Boston's Old State House Museum.

# Stick to a neutral color palette.

Pick a neutral color combo and plan your outfits around it. For example, go with black and gray or navy and khaki. Choose solid-color pieces in simple, versatile styles. This will allow you to mix-and-match each item you bring, which will make for more outfits. Also, if you bring neutral, solid-color pieces "you are less likely to get tired of wearing the items you bring, plus no one will notice if you wear the same item multiple times," says Kirshan Murphy, style advisor and founder of Theprofessionalgent.com. So instead of bringing patterned clothing, add pops of color and pattern with accessories like jewelry, scarves, belts, and ties. They can make an outfit look completely different from one day to the next.

Even if you don't normally wear a watch (perhaps you check the time on your cellphone), consider wearing one on your trip even if it's one that's strictly for pleasure. To make the most of your vacation you'll want to keep track of the time! It will come in handy, especially if you're traveling overseas and aren't using your cellphone regularly. Wear one that's neutral enough to go

Packing mix-and-match neutrals will give you the most flexible travel wardrobe.

with all of the outfits you bring with you.

While you may want to bring a few new items with you on your trip, now is not the best time to experiment with a completely new wardrobe. It's also not the ideal time to drag things out from the back of your closet that you never wear. Chances are, you don't wear them for a reason! It's always a smart idea to bring clothes that are tried-and-true favorites, along with other items that are in current rotation in your wardrobe. But if you do buy something new for your trip or if you are considering bringing an item you don't typically wear, road test it first. Try it on and inspect it while stand-

Use jewelry, scarves, and other accessories to change up your outfits.

ing in front of a full-length mirror. Check that it fits and that you like the way it looks. If the item passes that test, try the item on as if you were going to go out in it. Build an outfit around it, figure out what undergarments you need to wear with it, choose complementary accessories. You don't want to arrive and discover you can't wear something you've brought with you because it doesn't look right with the shoes you packed or because you don't have the proper undergarments with you.

# Pack one dressy outfit.

In case you end up going out to a nice dinner or a show, you should always bring a dressy ensemble with you. It can be as simple as bringing along dressy accessories like jewelry, a bag, or scarf—hints of sparkle are always an easy way to kick an outfit up a notch. "Think chic yet comfortable," says Fascitelli. "Women can take a shift dress from day to night by switching flats to heels and a tote to a clutch." Makeup is also a great way to look instantly dressier, so don't forget to throw lipstick, blush, and mascara in your toiletry bag.

Men can take a collared shirt and a pair of slacks and amp them up "with a vest or jacket, a tie, and nice shoes like dress shoes or loafers," says Murphy. "Neatly roll your tie and stuff it inside your dress shoes to save space in your bag."

# Go easy on your feet.

You'll probably do lots of walking, so be sure to bring at least one pair of sturdy, comfortable shoes. Pick a muted, simple pair that can be worn with all of the clothes you pack. Converse sneakers, boat shoes like Sperry Top-Siders, and boots are all great unisex options. For women, a pair of ballet flats always works, and for men, driving shoes from a brand like Tod's are comfy yet stylish. Other brands to consider are Clarks, Ecco, Børn, and Josef Seibel.

No matter how tempting it may be, "leave your flip-flops at home," says Murphy. "They don't provide any support for your feet, and they're very limiting—it's hard to dress them up! Go with a simple leather sandal instead."

Comfortable ballet flats can take you from sightseeing to a night at the theater.

If you buy a new pair of shoes for your trip, don't just assume they will be stand up to the rigors of city walking, even if they felt great in the store. Make sure you break them in a bit and test them out before you leave. Uncomfortable shoes can easily derail your trip.

TIP

69

# Let your gadgets do the navigating.

Equip your smartphone or tablet with city-specific maps, apps, and guides. A quick search in the iTunes Store or Android Market will yield tons of options. Pick the ones you want and download them ahead of time. If you prefer to carry a city guide in hard copy, avoid choosing one that's big and bulky (if that's unavoidable, rip out the pages you plan to refer to that day and just take those), and familiarize yourself with it before you leave. You may find it helpful to flag points of interest.

# Pack for bad weather.

On city trips you'll be out and about walking a lot, so you definitely do not want to get caught in a sudden rain shower or cold spell without the proper gear! If the forecast says a lot of rain, you might want to bring a pair of rain boots or another type of waterproof shoe. But typically, a pair of shoes that will hold up in the rain and keep your feet dry will suffice. Stash an umbrella in your bag and if it's cold out, bring a rain coat, but in warmer months a lightweight windbreaker will do. Always bring a lightweight sweater or cardigan—fine-gauge knits like cashmere and wool blends are good go-tos.

# Avoid being pickpocketed.

No matter what city you're traveling to, tourists are always prime targets for pickpockets. So be smart about where you stash your valuables. Bags that you carry in front of you, like messenger and crossbody bags with secure closures, are good options. Just remember to place valuables like your wallet in harder-to-reach inside pockets, and use any outside pockets for things like maps, lip balm, and tissues.

If you're going to be in areas that are particularly crowded or notorious for pickpockets, carry your money, credit cards, and ID in a security pouch or money belt that you wear underneath your clothes. Look for versions with slash-proof straps like over-the-shoulder styles from Pacsafe. Eagle Creek and Magellan's both make belts with hidden zippered pockets that discreetly conceal cash.

Keep valuables that you won't be using day to day, such as expensive jewelry (although it's always best to just leave those items at home; flashy gems can attract thieves) and your passport in the hotel safe if one is available. Some hotels may store certain items for you.

Split up your valuables, too. For example, don't carry all your cash in your wallet. Leave some in the hotel safe and keep a small amount in your pants pocket (if you can stuff a few bills inside without worrying about them falling out). If you're bringing two credit cards, carry one in your wallet and stash the second in the hotel safe. That way if you are robbed, you won't lose everything.

It's also a good idea to attach a TSA-approved lock to your suitcases. They'll give you added peace of mind, from traveling to your destination to leaving your bag behind in the hotel. Even though your valuables will be stored in the safe, you don't want to give anyone the opportunity to rifle through your bag at any time.

## Packing List

- ☐ A day bag
- ☐ Dressy accessories
- ☐ Comfortable walking shoes
- ☐ Umbrella
- ☐ Security pouch or money bag

# Special Celebrations

WHETHER YOU'RE HEADED TO A DESTINATION WEDDING, GRADUATION, anniversary party, or a milestone birthday, you'll want to make sure you've covered all of your bases, from what to wear to the special event to how to transport your gift.

TIP
72

# Carry on any important outfits.

The last thing you want to happen is for your most important outfit to be trapped inside a checked bag that is lost or delayed! So pack your dress or suit, shoes, and any accessories, such as a tie, purse or jewelry, in your carry-on. "You will have the security of knowing they will arrive with you," says Karen Klopp, Founder of What-2WearWhere. However you pack your outfit, a good rule of thumb is to always keep the entire outfit together so you'll know exactly where everything is at all times.

When packing, consider these two bag options:

## Garment bag

If you prefer to carry a garment bag, place clothes wrapped in plastic (like the bags you get from the dry cleaner) on a hanger. Then loop accessories like a tie, necklace, or an evening bag with a shoulder strap around the hanger. Stash your shoes (in shoe bags if you have them) and any additional accessories at the bottom of the garment bag. If you're traveling by plane, ask the flight attendant if there is a closet where your garment bag can be stowed. If there isn't one, wait until the last minute to place your garment bag in the overhead compartment to make sure nothing is placed on top of it. Also, remember that a garment bag does count as one of your two allowed carry-ons. If you're traveling by car, hang the garment bag or lay it out flat across the back seat or in the front, with nothing on top of it.

Previous page: Newlyweds pose on a bridge over the Thames, in London.

### Hard-sided suitcase

Another option is to pack everything in a wheeled, carry-on size bag. "Use a flat, hard-sided suitcase," says Klopp. "Neatly fold each item and place them in individual plastic bags to minimize wrinkles." The less you smash items, the fewer wrinkles they will have, so pack delicate and wrinkle-prone items on top, and heavy items like shoes on the bottom. Consider packing folders like those from Eagle Creek, which protect clothing from wrinkles and help you pack hard-to-fold items like suit jackets neatly.

TIP
73

# Bring comfortable shoes.

No matter if you're headed to a formal event or a casual one, it's important to bring a pair of comfortable (yet stylish!) shoes as well. Especially if you're wearing heels or uncomfortable dress shoes to

---

## Lists & Last-Minute Checks

"Take the time to anticipate weather and wardrobe needs so that you will avoid added stress," says Klopp. Check the weather a week before, and again the day before you leave so that you're prepared for any last-minute changes. In addition to your outfit for the main event, make a list of additional activities, such as rehearsal dinners, and pack outfits for each.

"When you're in doubt about what to pack, check with friends to see what they plan to bring," says Klopp. Also, it's always a good idea to check with your hotel or host ahead of time to make sure that an iron or a steamer (if needed), will be available to you.

the event, you'll want a pair of comfortable flats to change into afterward. They can be more casual than your event shoes, but choose a versatile, simple pair that you can wear with all of the outfits you've brought with you. Make sure they're stylish enough to wear to activities surrounding the event, such as lunch or drinks with fellow guests. An easy way to ensure you won't forget them is to actually wear them while you're traveling to your destination.

Basic black ballet flats are great options for women—they go with everything, and are sleek enough to wear anywhere. Brands like Footzy Rolls (www.footzyrolls.com) and Dr. Scholl's make styles that roll up small enough to fit in an evening bag. They're not sturdy enough for extensive walking, but they can be lifesavers in a pinch. Men should consider bringing "loafers, oxfords, boat shoes, or stylish sneakers," says Kirshan Murphy, style advisor and founder of Theprofessionalgent.com.

Also, bring the proper footwear for any other planned activities, such as hikes or watersports.

Pack a day bag with a camera and some comfy shoes.

# Be prepared to share photos & videos while you're there.

These trips are about special moments, so absolutely bring along any gear you might want to capture them, from cameras to camcorders to tripods. Along with those items, it's a great idea to bring the necessary cord or laptop that will allow you to download and share pictures and videos at your destination. That way you'll be prepared if the host or hostess, or fellow guests, ask you to share them on the spot, perhaps to send to relatives who could not attend, or for use in a special project such as a slide show on the last night. It will also allow you to free up space on your memory card.

Now is the time to bring along your top-notch SLR camera or HD camcorder, so don't stress over whether or not to devote precious real estate in your suitcase to them and all of their accessories—within reason, of course. If it comes down to an extra lens that might make an okay picture amazing, or yet another pair of pants that you probably won't wear, keep the lens and ditch the pants! If you do bring an SLR, you may also want to bring a small point-and-shoot camera that can fit into a purse or pocket.

# Ship gifts before you go.

If you're giving a gift that is heavy, fragile, or large, consider shipping it ahead of time, either to your destination or the recipient's home (they most likely will appreciate not having to lug it as well!).

*Left:* If you're flying, don't put wrapped gifts in your carry-on; TSA officers may unwrap them. Pack supplies and wrap gifts when you arrive. *Right:* Example of a TSA-approved lock—look for the diamond-shaped logo.

This will free up space in your suitcase, and will be one less item you have to keep track of. Another option is to purchase the gift after you've arrived. But this should only be done if you know exactly what you are going to purchase, and when and where you are going to purchase it, before you arrive. So do your research—you don't want to be hunting for the perfect gift at the very last minute!

If you prefer to travel with your gift, it's best to put it in a secure place that will stay with you at all times. When traveling by plane, pack it in your carry-on *unwrapped*—TSA rules allow for officers to unwrap gifts at security checkpoints if deemed necessary. You can always bring a gift bag or wrapping paper with you (folded and placed flat inside your suitcase) to use once you've reached your destination. If you must pack the gift in your checked luggage, it can be wrapped, just make sure it is packed properly in a bag with a TSA-approved lock.

Even if you're shipping your gift ahead of time or afterwards, "it's best to arrive with a special something in hand," says Klopp. Consider bringing a small, easy-to-pack token gift or a nice card.

## Packing List

- ☐ Clothing and accessories for the main event
- ☐ One pair of comfortable shoes
- ☐ Camera
- ☐ Camera cords
- ☐ Token gift or card

# Honeymoons

"YOU HAVE ATTENDED TO EVERY SMALL DETAIL OF THE WEDDING, AND that should carry over to the honeymoon," says Klopp. So don't slack off when prepping for your trip! Prepare thoroughly—and well in advance—to ensure a wonderful, stress-free trip as newlyweds.

TIP

76

# Invest in a set of high-quality luggage.

"It's a time for new beginnings, so you may want to invest in new, coordinated pieces of luggage," says Klopp. Plus, because you're likely to be staying in luxury hotels, you might want to upgrade your luggage.

Since you're splurging, do your research and choose a set of luggage you love and that suits your needs as a couple. Opt for top-notch, lightweight bags that are easy to maneuver and will last forever. Tumi and Bric's make extremely durable and lightweight bags that are ultrastylish and come in sleek colors, materials, and patterns. Investing in just one piece of luggage? Go for a carry-on—it's less likely to get dirty or damaged while traveling, and it's the bag that will be with you most of the time.

If you're leaving on your trip shortly after your wedding, pack your bags ahead of time so that you can enjoy your wedding without having to worry about taking on the task of packing immediately after the festivities. You will be able to just grab your bags and go!

Previous page: Strolling along the Seine in Paris.

# Assemble comfortable yet put-together outfits.

Think unfussy ensembles that can easily be dressed up or down. You want to be comfortable, but you also don't want to have to worry about whether or not you are dressed appropriately for certain settings, such as upscale restaurants or bars. Also, you'll appreciate having carefully planned your outfits when flipping through your photos together later, and sharing them with friends and family!

## On the plane

"For both men and women, layering is always a good idea, even in the summer, because planes and hotels can be chilly," says Klopp. On the plane, scarves, fine-gauge knit sweaters, and casual blazers are great ways to ward off chills. For women, denim or leggings and a solid-color T-shirt, paired with simple pair of ballet flats or flat boots always works. For men, roomy (but not baggy!) jeans or khakis and a nice tee or polo shirt paired with loafers or canvas sneakers will keep you comfy but stylish.

## While you're there

Bring simple pieces that can easily be dressed up or down to wear throughout the trip. Avoid wrinkle-prone items like silk, or fussy items that you will constantly have to readjust. Jersey dresses, cotton tees, black pants, cashmere sweaters and dark jeans with a clean finish are all great options to consider. If you're traveling to a hot climate, instead of your ripped cutoff shorts, consider a pair that's dressier, says Kirshan Murphy, style advisor and founder of Theprofessionalgent.com. "You can find shorts for both men

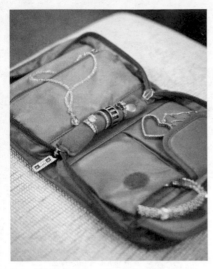

and women in nice fabrics that can easily be worn to dinner or an evening out."

Accessories are great ways to dress up, and get more mileage out of, your outfits—plus, they don't take up too much room in your suitcase. For women, a pair of sparkly sandals, a great piece of jewelry, or an elegant clutch will do the trick. Men can use a tie, cuff links, a belt, a pocket square, or a tie bar to instantly add a dressy element to their looks.

Keep delicate jewelry protected with a soft organizer like this one.

Lastly, don't forget loungewear! Your honeymoon is a time to relax and unwind with your new spouse, so you'll want to bring plenty of clothes to wear when you're headed to the spa or lazing around your hotel room. Yoga pants, sweats, shorts, tanks, and T-shirts all work—just leave anything super ratty at home!

TIP
78

# Protect delicate items.

"For jewelry, use a roll-up organizer and keep it with you in your carry-on luggage or purse," says Klopp. A soft-sided organizer is easy to pack and will protect your jewelry from being damaged, lost, or stolen. There are tons of different styles, from durable nylon to high-end leather, to suit your needs. Just make sure that the roll securely closes and keeps everything in its place. Pop men's jewelry, tie bars, and cuff links in the case as well.

Place delicate lingerie in protective bags to prevent rips and snags. Consider investing in cotton bags that zip closed (they're reusable and can be thrown in the washing machine), or in a pinch just pop them in a Ziploc bag!

It's best to pack evening purses and shoes in individual bags as well. Cotton bags are great, but Ziploc bags or recycled plastic grocery bags also work.

TIP

## 79

# Bring a tripod for hands-free picture taking.

In addition to a camera and a camcorder, bring along a tripod. It will allow you to take pictures as newlyweds even when no one is around to help. JOBY's GorrillaPod is a super-versatile option (www.joby.com). It has flexible legs that you can adjust individually to accommodate uneven surfaces. You can even wrap them around a railing or a tree branch.

A tripod will help you get shots of both of you enjoying your trip together.

## Packing List

- ☐ Fine-gauge knit sweater
- ☐ Jewelry and jewelry case
- ☐ Lingerie
- ☐ Loungewear
- ☐ Tripod

# Spa Vacations

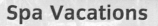

TAKING A SPA VACATION? LUCKY YOU! NO MATTER IF YOU'RE TRAVELING alone or with your closest girlfriends, don't forget that the point of this kind of trip is to unwind and de-stress. "Whatever you can do to prepare in advance and relax before you even start is a great idea," says Susie Ellis, President of SpaFinder, Inc. It's easy to overlook, but be sure that travel to your destination, whether it's by car or plane, is as comfortable as possible so you can start off in a relaxed mindset. So do bring along your favorite pillow and travel blanket. You might want to also bring along earplugs and an eye mask, especially if you're going on a long flight.

Also keep in mind that there are typically two types of spas: resort spas (located within resorts) and destination spas (a lodging facility where spa treatments and activities are the main focal points). Generally, you'll want to pack more for a resort spa than you will for a destination spa. Both types of spas are covered in this section.

TIP

# 80

# Use a tote or a backpack as one of your carry-on bags.

"One thing that people always forget is a tote to carry items from their room to whatever activity they're going to be doing," says Ellis. For most activities, a canvas or nylon tote will suffice, but if you will be doing any hiking (especially if it's extensive), you might want to bring a backpack. Either bag can double as your personal bag on the plane.

In addition to your tote or backpack, rolling duffels and soft-sided suitcases are both great options.

Previous page: Luxuriating at a spa in Ubud, Bali.

Bring a tote that you can use to carry around the spa once you arrive. If you're flying, pick something that you can use as a carry-on bag.

TIP
81

# Before you leave, find out what items the spa provides.

This will take the guesswork out of deciding what to bring. "Most resort and destination spas will provide basic toiletries, yoga mats, robes, slippers, and water bottles," says Ellis. "Definitely bring a toothbrush and toothpaste, and if you're a yoga devotee and have a favorite mat, then certainly bring that. And although water will be provided, consider bringing along an eco-friendly, reusable water bottle." Consider one that filters water as you drink; two companies that make lightweight, durable versions are Hydros (www.hydros bottle.com) and Bobble (www.waterbobble.com).

"If you do forget something, or prefer to purchase certain items once you get there, almost every spa nowadays has a gift shop where you can find anything you need, down to toothbrushes, workout clothes, and even socks," says Ellis. "So the most important things to bring are your hiking shoes and athletic shoes because they're the hardest things to purchase while you're there."

Additional things Ellis suggests to keep in mind:

- Avoid bringing clothes that have to be dry cleaned. Stick to items that can be hand washed or thrown in a washing machine if necessary.
- Pack plenty of socks and underwear, as you will be changing them quite a bit.
- Bring at least two bathing suits with you—a nice one for relaxing in the pool or sauna, and one that you don't mind wearing to treatments where it might get mud or salt on it.
- Unless you're planning on a dressy dinner or night out, leave your super-fancy clothes at home. Especially at a destination spa—sometimes people may opt to dress up for dinner on the last night, but in general the dress code is casual. At some spas you can even attend meals in your bathrobe!

TIP
82

# Plan your activities ahead of time.

Of course this doesn't have to be set in stone, but it will ensure you bring along the proper clothing and gear for each activity. If you're traveling with a group, it will also help to avoid potential disagreements. Before heading out, discuss the itinerary with each person in your group. Go over all of the gear that will be needed in order to participate so that you're all on the same page and no one gets left out. Have each person weigh in so that everyone feels involved in the planning process. Lastly, be sure everyone is aware of, and happy with, all of the activities that have been mapped out. The more you can do to cut down on spats (or confusion) during the trip, the better!

TIP

## 83

# Do bring electronics, but use them sparingly.

Although it sounds counterintuitive, pack your cellphone, laptop, and any other items you typically use on a daily basis. "Hopefully you will not use them, but if you have to they will be readily available as opposed to having to go to the business center, which can potentially cause more stress," says Ellis. "Items may be in use, or they may not have something that you need." Just remember to try to use them as little as possible, and set time limits for yourself if needed. For example, if you need to check in with work, allow yourself only 30 minutes to do so. The less plugged-in you are, the more you will get out of your spa vacation or girlfriend getaway!

Don't forget extra memory cards for your camera.

Also, "consider taking a book you find inspirational," suggests Ellis. Whether it be a paperback or a download on your Kindle, it will help keep you in the spirit of this type of trip.

## Packing List

- ☐ A day bag (backpack or tote)
- ☐ Sun protection (sunscreen, hat, and sunglasses)
- ☐ Athletic shoes
- ☐ Cellphone
- ☐ An inspirational book

# Vacation Rentals

THERE ARE ALL DIFFERENT KINDS OF VACATION RENTALS, INCLUDING apartments, condos, cabins, beach houses, and more! "Staying in a vacation rental makes it possible for families and groups to spread out and have access to amenities that can make their trip more comfortable," says Alexis de Belloy, Vice President of Home-Away. "Having the details laid out can save travelers time and money in the long run!"

TIP
84

# Do your research.

"It's important to keep in mind that unlike hotels, no two vacation rentals are exactly the same," says Belloy. "The number one rule when determining what to pack for a vacation rental is to talk to the homeowner and determine what is and isn't already offered. Find out what will be available to you, from washing machines and kitchen utensils to board games."

Have a list of necessities handy when you're taking inventory with the owner to make sure you're not forgetting anything. You'll also want to check that there are enough of certain items like bed linens and bath towels to go around. "Having the knowledge of what's included in your rental may make it possible to lighten your luggage and save money on exorbitant baggage fees if you're flying to your destination," says de Belloy.

Here's a list of items you may want to inquire about:

- Eating utensils (knives, forks, spoons)
- Cooking utensils (spatula, chef knife, mixing spoons, strainer, tongs, grater, measuring cup, mixing bowls)
- Dishes (plates, bowls, drinking glasses, mugs)
- Appliances (microwave, oven, stove, coffee maker, blender)
- Corkscrew
- Cookware (pots and pans)

Previous page: Pebble Beach, California.

- Bakeware (cookie sheet, casserole dish, cake pan)
- Paper products (paper towels, paper plates)
- Bed linens (sheets, blankets, pillows, pillowcases)
- Hangers
- Bath towels
- Hand towels
- Toilet paper
- Basic toiletries (shampoo, conditioner, hand soap, body lotion)
- Toys and games (playing cards, board games)
- Television
- DVD player
- DVDs

Once you've determined what you need to bring, be smart about whether it's best to bring them with you or buy them once you arrive. If an item is expensive and not incredibly bulky, like a travel-size blow-dryer, bring it with you. If an item is bulky and inexpensive versions are readily available, like an extra towel or cookie sheet, consider purchasing those when you get there.

Headed somewhere secluded? Ask the homeowner for a list of shops in the area, and don't just assume that the stores have the items you plan to purchase. Call ahead to make sure the items you need are in stock.

Find out before you go what linens come with the house, and what you'll need to provide.

# Bring groceries.

"One of the best things about vacation rentals is the flexibility of having your own kitchen," says de Belloy. "Some homeowners will offer to do the grocery shopping for their guests ahead of time, but typically travelers should anticipate having to buy their own groceries."

If you're traveling by car and you have room in your trunk, pack nonperishable items before you leave; that way you'll have snacks

If you're traveling by car, bring some groceries to the house with you. That way you'll spend less of your vacation time at the grocery store.

on hand if you're hungry when you get there, and you won't have to spend as much precious vacation time grocery shopping. You also might save some money—stores in resort areas often have higher prices than your local store back home. If you have room in your car, pack a bag of kitchen basics you know you will want to use right away, such as olive oil, salt, pepper, coffee, and sugar (of course, check with the owner first to make sure these items won't be provided). Also consider bringing items like dried pasta, peanut butter, jelly, rice, popcorn, cereal, and any other staples you and your family uses on a regular basis. Plan to stop and get items like milk and eggs when you arrive. Reusable grocery bags, like colorful ones from Baggu (www.baggubag.com) or RuMe (www.rumebags.com), are incredibly useful to have on hand. If you're traveling by plane, stash a few reusable grocery bags in your luggage and plan to stop at the grocery store once you arrive.

Remember to only buy food that can be prepared with the tools that will be provided in the kitchen or that you plan to purchase.

TIP
**86**

# Don't forget toiletries.

Most vacation rentals do not provide toiletries, so plan to bring your own. If you're traveling by plane, bring enough to get you through the first 2 or 3 days, and buy larger bottles after you arrive

Most rentals don't provide toiletries, so don't forget to bring your own.

if needed. Bringing small amounts of the necessities will allow you to get settled before having to rush right out and buy more. Also, you will be able to take inventory before heading to the store as well—there may be some items on hand that you didn't know would be available. Or on the flip side, there might be some other items you thought would be available that aren't. If you're traveling by car, you'll have more space and won't have to adhere to TSA rules, so feel free to bring along all of the toiletries you need for your entire stay.

TIP

87

# Think about bringing recreational items.

"The type of vacation rental you're staying in and where it's located may entice you to bring specific items along with you that you might not have thought of otherwise," says de Belloy. "For example, if you're staying in a cabin that has a fireplace or an outdoor fire pit, consider bringing your favorite blanket to cozy up with and supplies for making s'mores with your kids. For a beach house rental, you might want to bring your kids' favorite toys and a couple of beach mats," says de Belloy. "But always remember to check with the homeowner first as they may already provide family-friendly extras so you don't have to bring them with you."

Dollar stores are a great place to stock up on cheap entertainment items for kids. You'll likely find games, puzzles, balls, beach toys, sidewalk chalk, coloring books, bubbles, and more. It will help keep the troops entertained and you can always leave them behind when you leave if you need room in your suitcase for souvenirs.

## Packing List

- ☐ A list of all of the items available to you
- ☐ A list of all of the items you need to buy upon arrival
- ☐ Toiletries (at least 2 days' worth)
- ☐ Reusable grocery bags
- ☐ Special recreational items

# Traveling with Pets

WHEN TRAVELING WITH ANIMALS IT'S EXTREMELY IMPORTANT TO DO extensive research ahead of time, particularly when traveling by plane. Fees and rules vary depending on the airline, size and breed of pet, weather conditions, time of year, destination, and more. With so many guidelines, traveling with your pet can be confusing, but the more prepared you are, the smoother your trip will go. Call your airline or visit their website for the most accurate, up-to-date information. Depending on how in-depth the airline's website is, they may direct you to the U.S. Department of Agriculture's Veterinary Services for further information, but it's the best (and easiest) place to start.

If you're traveling internationally, each country has its own set of rules, so contact the embassy or consulate of the country you are visiting to determine regulations and required documentation.

Here's an overview of guidelines you should be aware of when traveling by plane:

- All required fees must be paid at airport check-in.
- The number of pets allowed on each flight varies per plane. So the sooner you let your airline know you will be traveling with a pet, the better! Always reconfirm 24 to 48 hours before your departure.
- Your pet must be at least 8 weeks old.
- Your pet must remain in its carrier at all times during the flight.
- Your pet must be able to comfortably stand, lie down, and turn around in its carrier.
- In order for your pet to travel with you in the cabin, the carrier must be small enough to fit underneath the seat in front of you (this varies by plane, so check with your airline). If the carrier will not fit, it must be checked.
- If you carry your pet on the plane with you, the carrier counts as one of your two allowed carry-ons.
- In addition to cats and dogs, domesticated birds, rabbits, and other animals may be allowed on the plane. Check with your airline and the USDA for more information.

Previous page: Playing fetch on a beach on Martha's Vineyard.

- Some airlines will not accept pets as checked luggage during certain weather conditions and times of the year, as extreme hot and cold temperatures may be harmful to your pet.

- There are special restrictions as to during what weather conditions snub-nosed breeds (such as pugs, bulldogs, Boston terriers, Shih Tzus and Persian cats) are allowed to fly.

- Hawaii has strict regulations (including a required quarantine period) in place regarding pets being brought into the state, and therefore airlines have special rules in place as well. If you're headed there, in addition to checking with your airline, be sure to also check with the Hawaii Department of Agriculture.

- Your airline, or the state or country to which you are traveling, may require your pet to travel with a health certificate issued by a licensed, accredited veterinarian (if you're traveling by car you should also bring along health documentation for your pet, especially if you're crossing state lines).

- Many of these guidelines, including additional fees, do not apply to service animals, so check your airline's website if traveling with one.

TIP

88

# Choose the proper carrier.

Once you have determined your mode of travel, and if your pet will travel in the cabin or has to be checked on the plane, it's time to pick a carrier!

If your pet is traveling in the plane's cabin (or by car):

"Choose a secure, soft-sided carrier that has solid zippers, a waterproof bottom, and adequate ventilation," says Susan Smith, president and owner of Pet Travel, Inc. Size absolutely matters! Airlines won't let you bring your pet on the plane if it's crammed into a too-small carrier, so make sure your pet can move around in it comfortably and naturally. "The weight of the bag is also important. Especially if you are flying internationally, your pet may be weighed in the bag, and there are maximum limits set for carry-on luggage."

There are many different styles, colors, and brands of carriers out there with all sorts of handy features, so shop around to find the one that best suits you and your pet's needs. "At Pettravel-store.com, we carry three different kinds of carriers," says Smith. "Sherpa, because the brand is very well known and their bags are well made; Bergan because they make great, utilitarian bags; and SturdiBag because their bags are very lightweight, they allow for extra height, and they're designed with plastic ribbing so that you can squish the carrier down to get it underneath a seat without crushing your pet."

If your pet is traveling as checked luggage:

Look for a kennel that adheres to USDA guidelines. "Just like a soft-sided carrier, your pet must be able to move about freely, and the crate needs be sturdy, have adequate ventilation, a waterproof bottom, and a spring-loaded door, since many pets are very adept at reaching up and opening latches!" says Smith. "It also has to have live animal stickers and water and food bowls attached to the inside of the door that are accessible from the outside."

Don't forget to line the kennel with absorbent material or bedding, such as shredded newspapers, and to mark the crate with a THIS END UP note, as well as your pet's name and your name and cellphone number.

Most airlines require a health certificate and a statement (written and signed by the owner) indicating any special feeding instructions, as well as the date and time when your pet was last given food and water.

TIP

89

# Secure your pet in the car.

If you decide to bring your pet along on your next car trip make sure your pet is buckled up, too! While it may be tempting to let your pet move around freely, it can be extremely dangerous. In an accident your pet could be fatally thrown from the car or become a dangerous projectile to human passengers. A roaming pet could distract the driver or crawl under the gas and brake pedals and cause a devastating accident. It's also dangerous to let your dog ride with his or her head hanging out of the window. Debris can cause injury, especially when traveling on the highway at increased speeds, or the opening may be big enough for an excited pet to get out (or fall out) of the car.

So with all of these factors in mind, it's a lot safer for your pet (and for everyone in the car) if he or she is securely fastened, either to the seat itself or in a carrier that's tethered to the seat! There are lots of different accessories and carriers that will do the trick while keeping your pet comfortable and happy while along for the ride. Here are several options to consider:

- **Seat belt harnesses** fasten to the seat belt in your car to limit your pet's mobility. Look for one with lots of padding that won't dig into your pet's chest or shoulders.
- **Kennel restraints** are straps that loop around your hard or soft-sided carrier to secure it to the seat.
- **Car seats** for your pet attach securely to seat. They come in all different shapes and sizes, with various levels of padding. Some soft-sided carriers double as carriers you can use out of the car. There are versions for both the back and front seats, and they have straps that either slip over the seat to keep it secure or that tether the car seat to the seat belt. Go for a model that has a collar that's already attached to the car seat to keep your pet secure.
- **Booster seats** are elevated versions of car seats. They allow your pet to see clearly out the window while staying safe. If your dog likes to stick his or her head out of the window, this is a great alternative!
- **Vehicle barriers** restrict your pet to certain areas of the car, such as the back seat or the cargo hold. There are many different versions that are made of all types of materials, from steel bars to soft netting. They're great for securing larger animals.

All of these options are readily available at local pet stores (Petsmart, Petco, Pet Supermarket). You can also find them online,.

---

## Pet ID

...............................................................................................

"When you're traveling, it doesn't do any good to have your home phone on your pet's collar because you're not there," says Smith. If your pet's day-to-day collar does not list your cellphone number, attach a temporary tag with it listed in case of any emergencies. If your pet is traveling by crate in the cargo hold, make sure your contact information is attached to the outside of the crate as well.

---

but with so many different options out there you may want to actually visit the store and bring your pet along, too. A store employee can give advice and recommendations to help you pick the one that best suits you and your pet's needs. Also, you can test it out on your pet (and in your car!) to make sure it fits properly and comfortably.

TIP
**90**

# Bring a photo of your pet with you.

If the photo is taken right before you leave on your trip, it ensures that both you and your pet look the same in the photo as you do while you're traveling. In an old photo your pet could be a different size, its hair could be cut differently, and so on. "It will be tremendously helpful in terms of identification if your pet is lost," says Smith. Bring along a printed copy of the photo, but also have a digital copy available in case it's helpful to e-mail a copy to the police or animal control.

TIP

**91**

# Don't pack a lot of food.

Unless your pet eats food not readily available in stores, it's best to bring enough food (including treats!) and water for use en route, and plan to buy more when you reach your destination. If you're traveling by car, you can pack as much food as space permits.

Always bring along portable water and food bowls. Popware (www.popwareforpets.com) and Outward Hound (www.kyjen. com) both make easy-to-use collapsible versions.

Pet food takes up a lot of space. Unless your pet's food is difficult to find, pack just enough for the trip.

TIP
92

# Make sure your pet is comfortable.

The American Veterinary Medical Association recommends that you do not sedate your pet when traveling by air, because doing so may increase the risk of heart and respiratory problems. Even if you're traveling by car it can be risky! There are however, plenty of non-narcotic things you can do for your pet to take the edge off.

Follow Smith's tricks to keep your pet happy and calm while on the go.

### Purchase a carrier well in advance

"You want your pet to be as familiar as possible with their carrier before your trip, so encourage your pet to spend time in it, take a nap in it. Leave the door open, put treats and their favorite toys in it," says Smith. "Also, put your pet in the carrier and take it to a dog park a couple of times. That way your pet will associate the carrier with something fun!"

### Pack the carrier with something familiar

Bring along your pet's favorite soft toy, and "if your pet has a bed with a zippered cover, take that off and put it in the carrier," says Smith. "Another thing I like to suggest is to take a T-shirt and rub it against your chest and put that in the carrier. That way your pet will have your scent with them, which is very comforting to your pet!"

## *Restrict your pet's view*

"If your pet is in a bag, carrier, or crate, keep the privacy flaps down, or if you're in the car put a blanket over one side of it," says Smith. Of course make sure the bag is still well ventilated, but just don't allow your pet to look out and see what's going on around them—or other people. "It will just add to their nervousness and hyperactivity."

## *Consider using a pet calmer*

"They're all-natural and are widely used in the industry to calm nervous and anxious pets. They won't put your pet to sleep, but will calm him or her down," says Smith. "Ark Natural makes a great one called Happy Traveler." It comes in a pill form that you can bury in your pet's favorite treat (www.arknaturals.com). You can also buy pet calmers in chewable form.

## *Bring a leash*

"No matter how well your pet obeys you at home, it can be unpredictable while traveling, so you always want to bring a good leash!" says Smith. Get in the habit of bringing a leash whenever you and your pet leave home, even if you're just driving a few blocks away from home.

Don't forget your pet's favorite toys, leash, bags for cleaning up waste, and some treats.

TIP

**93**

# Line your pet's carrier with absorbent pads.

You always want to be prepared for any messes! In addition to extra plastic bags, it's also a good idea to bring several absorbent pads (such as Four Paws' Wee-Wee Pads) made especially for pets. A great way to carry them without taking up extra space in your luggage is to "stack two or three in the bottom of the carrier so that if your pet soils one of them, you can just slide it out and there will be a fresh one underneath!" says Smith. Even if you're traveling by car and plan to stop for frequent food and bathroom breaks, it's still a good idea—you'll be prepared for unexpected mishaps.

## Packing List

- ☐ Tag with your cellphone number on it
- ☐ A recent photo of you and your pet
- ☐ Portable water and food bowls
- ☐ Your pet's favorite toy
- ☐ Any necessary medications
- ☐ A good leash

# Bringing Home Special Purchases

KEEPSAKES ARE WONDERFUL REMINDERS OF ADVENTURES AWAY FROM home. Whether it's an investment piece, a token gift for a loved one, or a unique find for yourself, these mementoes can be enjoyed long after your trip. So you'll want to make sure that your items arrive back home intact and without any damage.

Think about the kinds of things you may want to buy along the way. If you know you normally like to buy things while you're traveling—and especially if you're going with an eye for something fragile, such as glass or a piece of art—consider bringing some packing materials, such as bubble wrap, tissue paper, and plastic coverings, in your suitcase. You can also call ahead (your hotel is a good place to start, or you can try inquiring at a local shop) to your destination city and find out what packing materials are typically available, and whether they are complementary with purchase or you need to buy them separately. If you bring materials with you that you don't wind up needing, you can just throw them away to free up space in your bag on the return trip home. But even if an item isn't particularly fragile, it never hurts to have a little added protection.

Also, even if you're not typically a shopper or you're a frugal, extremely practical traveler, don't go with the mind-set that you will buy nothing. You may just come across something that you absolutely love and have to have. With these things in mind, you should always plan ahead to ensure that you don't have to say "no" to that one-of-a-kind find.

TIP
94

# Ship items if possible.

Especially if items are awkwardly shaped, heavy, or fragile, check to see if shipping is an option. It will save you the hassle of figuring out how best to get it home intact. If you're traveling overseas and are having something shipped from a store, make sure the VAT, or sales tax, is deducted from your purchase. This will help alleviate the shipping costs.

Previous page: ABC Carpet & Home, in New York City.

TIP

**95**

# Have an empty tote, just in case.

It's always a good idea to pack an extra bag in your suitcase just for souvenirs. Even if you don't set out with plans to buy something, you may come across an item or two that you want to buy, and you don't want to be forced to pass on something because you don't have room for it in your bag. Reusable nylon bags are great because they fold flat and are very compact. If you want to invest in a sturdier bag, consider a canvas tote or a zippered nylon style from a brand like Longchamp. Many luggage companies also make nylon totes that fold up.

Even if you have to check the extra bag, the additional baggage fees may prove more economical than shipping costs, especially when traveling abroad.

TIP

**96**

# Wrap breakable items carefully.

When purchasing items from a store, make sure that they wrap each item well, in tissue paper or bubble wrap. Use your clothes for extra cushioning—soft cotton items like T-shirts work particularly

If you didn't bring any packing supplies, you can wrap delicate items in clothing to protect them in your suitcase.

If you know you'll be shopping on your trip, throw some bubble wrap in your suitcase.

well. Keep in mind that you may have to unwrap these items at security, so if items are wrapped but are not breakable, pack them in your checked luggage.

If you know you are traveling to a place that is known for certain fragile items, such as handblown glass or hand-carved wooden figures, you may want to consider bringing some tissue paper and bubble wrap with you in your suitcase. Yes, the supplies will take up room in your bag, but what better way to reserve space in your suitcase for souvenirs than with supplies that will protect them on the way home?

TIP
**97**

# Know which items will get past Customs.

When traveling overseas, check the Customs and Border Protection's website (www.cbp.gov) for a detailed list of the current restricted items before you go. This will help to avoid having any of your souvenirs confiscated. People often get stopped for attempting to take home certain food items (especially when returning from Italy!), so make sure you're well versed in what's allowable and what isn't. Note that if you're traveling to or from Hawaii from the mainland United States, there a number of agricultural restrictions in place even though you're staying within the same country. Generally, packaged products (macadamia nuts, coffee) will make it through, but fresh produce and flowers will not. Be sure to educate yourself before you purchase something with the intent of bringing it home with you.

TIP
**98**

# Flatten or roll art.

Pack items like canvas sketches or photographs where they can lie flat in your suitcase. Don't put them on the very bottom because the weight of items piled on top can be damaging. Plus, the handle bars can cause dents. Instead, place items on the very top along with the rest of your delicate items—they'll create a soft cushion.

Cover them with a paper or plastic bag, bubble wrap or tissue paper. If the piece can be rolled easily and without causing damage, consider placing it in a poster tube. Always remember to ask if these items are available to you wherever you purchase the art. In a pinch, use things like newspapers and plastic grocery bags as protection.

If you purchase a poster or print, ask the shop or gallery where you made your purchase for a poster tube to help protect it.

TIP
99

# Take special care with wine bottles.

Don't wrap bottles of wine in your sweaters and cross your fingers that they won't leak all over your suitcase! Ship them whenever possible, but if you know you're likely to bring wine home with you, consider grabbing a few bags specially made to protect vino. Companies like WineSkin (www.wineskin.net) make double-sealed, leak-proof sleeves that will protect your bottles during transport.

TIP

100

# Unpack & repack
# your suitcase.

Never try to cram your souvenirs around what's already in your suitcase. When it's time to head home, take everything out (yes, everything!) and completely repack, paying special attention to fragile items. Not only will this help keep your finds from being damaged, but it will also allow you to stay organized.

# MASTER PACKING LIST

**CLOTHING**

- ☐ Sweaters/cardigans
- ☐ T-shirts
- ☐ Short-sleeve tops
- ☐ Long-sleeve tops
- ☐ Pants
- ☐ Shorts
- ☐ Skirts
- ☐ Underwear
- ☐ Bras
- ☐ Everyday socks
- ☐ Activity-specific socks (wool, sport, moisture-wicking, extra-thick)
- ☐ Sock liners
- ☐ Dress socks
- ☐ Formal wear (dress, suit, heels, tie, dress shoes)
- ☐ Suit
- ☐ Collared shirt
- ☐ Undershirt
- ☐ Collar stays
- ☐ Lightweight jacket or blazer
- ☐ Loungewear
- ☐ Rain jacket
- ☐ Rain pants
- ☐ Coat
- ☐ Base layers
- ☐ Gym shorts
- ☐ Sports bra
- ☐ Workout shirt
- ☐ Bathing suit
- ☐ Beach coverup

## MASTER PACKING LIST

- ☐ Pajamas
- ☐ Insulating vest

## SHOES
- ☐ Hiking boots
- ☐ Athletic shoes
- ☐ Flip-flops
- ☐ Water shoes
- ☐ Comfortable flat shoes
- ☐ Waterproof shoes
- ☐ Shower shoes
- ☐ Heels
- ☐ Work shoes
- ☐ Fashion sneakers

## ACCESSORIES
- ☐ Winter scarf
- ☐ Winter hat
- ☐ Winter gloves
- ☐ Sun hat
- ☐ Sunglasses
- ☐ Watch (waterproof if necessary)
- ☐ Jewelry (earrings, bracelets, necklaces, rings)
- ☐ Pocket square
- ☐ Fashion scarf
- ☐ Necktie(s)
- ☐ Tie bar
- ☐ Cuff links
- ☐ Eye glasses
- ☐ Day bag
- ☐ Empty reusable shopping bag(s)
- ☐ Belt
- ☐ Security pouch or money belt
- ☐ Coin pouch

- ☐ Beach tote
- ☐ Headband
- ☐ Hair elastics

## TOILETRIES

- ☐ Hand sanitizer
- ☐ Handi Wipes
- ☐ Shampoo
- ☐ Conditioner
- ☐ Toothpaste
- ☐ Toothbrush
- ☐ Floss
- ☐ Fingernail clippers
- ☐ Tweezers
- ☐ Contact lens solution
- ☐ Face cleanser
- ☐ Sunscreen
- ☐ Sunscreen towelettes
- ☐ Soap
- ☐ Lip balm
- ☐ Makeup
- ☐ Lotion
- ☐ Eye drops
- ☐ Cotton balls
- ☐ Q-tips
- ☐ Shaving cream
- ☐ Razor
- ☐ Razor blades
- ☐ Deodorant
- ☐ Feminine hygiene products
- ☐ Hairbrush
- ☐ Comb
- ☐ Insect repellent

## MASTER PACKING LIST

### PERSONAL ITEMS
- ☐ Eyeglasses
- ☐ Eyeglass case
- ☐ Eyeglass cleaning cloth
- ☐ Contact lenses
- ☐ Contact lens case
- ☐ Wallet
- ☐ Credit card(s)
- ☐ Debit card

### WELLNESS
- ☐ Allergy medicine
- ☐ Contraceptives
- ☐ Cold medicine
- ☐ Nausea medication
- ☐ Diarrhea medication
- ☐ Motion sickness medication
- ☐ Prescription medications
- ☐ Children's medications
- ☐ Vitamins
- ☐ First-aid kit
- ☐ Blister kit
- ☐ Immunity booster (Airborne, Emergen-C)
- ☐ Water sterilization tablets
- ☐ Malaria pills
- ☐ Earplugs
- ☐ Eye mask

### DOCUMENTS AND IDENTIFICATION
- ☐ Passport
- ☐ Copy of first page of passport
- ☐ Driver's license
- ☐ Visa(s)
- ☐ Vaccination certificates
- ☐ Medical insurance card

## GADGETS

- ☐ Cellphone
- ☐ Camera
- ☐ Camcorder
- ☐ Laptop
- ☐ Tablet (i.e., iPad)
- ☐ E-reader (i.e., Kindle)
- ☐ Extra batteries
- ☐ Flashlight
- ☐ Head lamp
- ☐ GPS
- ☐ Battery chargers
- ☐ USB cord
- ☐ Extension cord
- ☐ Power strip
- ☐ Outlet multiplier
- ☐ Tripod
- ☐ Travel alarm clock
- ☐ Electronic games (i.e., Nintendo DS)
- ☐ Portable DVD player
- ☐ Converter
- ☐ Adapter
- ☐ Travel steamer
- ☐ Backup charger or battery extender
- ☐ Cases/covers for gadgets (waterproof, if needed)
- ☐ Hairdryer
- ☐ Flatiron
- ☐ Curling iron
- ☐ Electric shaver
- ☐ Headphones
- ☐ MP3 player
- ☐ Extra memory card
- ☐ Extra film
- ☐ Binoculars

## MASTER PACKING LIST

### FOR YOUR KIDS
- ☐ Baby food/formula
- ☐ Bottle
- ☐ Diapers
- ☐ Diaper bag
- ☐ Changing pad
- ☐ Toys
- ☐ Art supplies
- ☐ Baby wipes
- ☐ Bib
- ☐ Clothing
- ☐ Plastic bags for soiled items
- ☐ Pacifier
- ☐ Snacks (food and drinks)
- ☐ Pillow
- ☐ Blanket
- ☐ Travel potty

### FOR YOUR PET
- ☐ Proper carrier
- ☐ Food
- ☐ Health certificate
- ☐ Tag or collar with your cellphone number listed
- ☐ Recent photo of you and your pet
- ☐ Collapsible water and food bowls
- ☐ Soft chew toys
- ☐ Wee-Wee Pads
- ☐ Leash
- ☐ Medication(s)
- ☐ List of special feeding instructions
- ☐ Pet calmer
- ☐ Plastic poop bags
- ☐ International travel documents

## FOR THE CAR
- ☐ Ice scraper
- ☐ Spare tire
- ☐ Registration and insurance documents
- ☐ First-aid kit
- ☐ Spare set of keys
- ☐ Cooler
- ☐ Jumper cables
- ☐ Spare fuses
- ☐ Roadside assistance numbers
- ☐ Rags
- ☐ Jack
- ☐ Basic tool kit
- ☐ Tire gauge
- ☐ Warning light or reflective triangles
- ☐ Flares
- ☐ Shovel
- ☐ Blanket
- ☐ Duct tape
- ☐ Bungee cord
- ☐ Tire chains
- ☐ Tow strap
- ☐ Nonperishable food
- ☐ Water
- ☐ Umbrella
- ☐ Fire extinguisher

## MISCELLANEOUS
- ☐ Clothing soap/detergent
- ☐ Sports equipment and gear (helmet, gloves, skis and ski boots, snowboard, goggles, hand warmers)
- ☐ Clothesline
- ☐ Umbrella

## Master Packing List

- ☐ Reading material (if you don't have an e-reader)
- ☐ Extra plastic bags
- ☐ List of emergency contact information
- ☐ Gift(s)
- ☐ Reusable water bottle
- ☐ Yoga mat
- ☐ Beach towels
- ☐ Quick-drying towel
- ☐ Travel pillow
- ☐ Travel blanket
- ☐ Guidebook
- ☐ Map(s)
- ☐ WineSkins
- ☐ Wet/dry bag
- ☐ Insulated bag
- ☐ Bed liner
- ☐ Sleeping bag
- ☐ Snacks (food and drinks)
- ☐ Swiss Army knife (in checked baggage)
- ☐ Small sewing kit
- ☐ TSA-approved lock

# Index